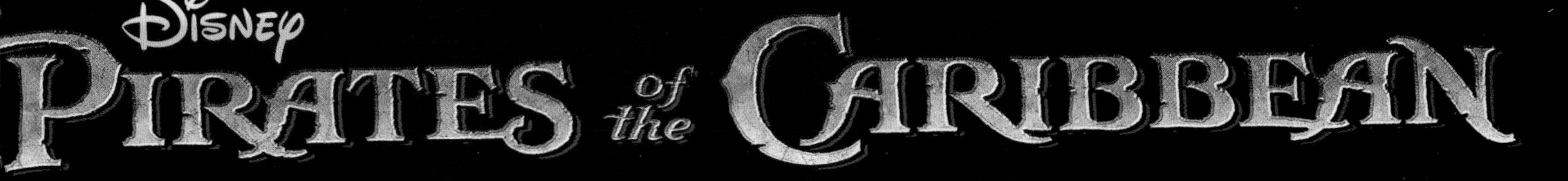

DEAD MEN TELL NO TALES

MUSIC FROM THE MOTION PICTURE SOUNDTRACK

ISBN 978-1-5400-0045-3

In Australia Contact:
Hal Leonard Australia Pty. Ltd.
4 Lentara Court
Cheltenham, Victoria, 3192 Australia
Email: ausadmin@halleonard.com.au

Visit Hal Leonard Online at
www.halleonard.com

10 DEAD MEN TELL NO TALES
12 SALAZAR
16 NO WOMAN HAS EVER HANDLED MY HERSCHEL
24 YOU SPEAK OF THE TRIDENT
26 KILL THE FILTHY PIRATE, I'LL WAIT
9 THE DYING GULL
46 THE BRIGHTEST STAR IN THE NORTH
32 TREASURE
38 MY NAME IS BARBOSSA
42 BEYOND MY BELOVED HORIZON

THE DYING GULL

Music by
GEOFF ZANELLI

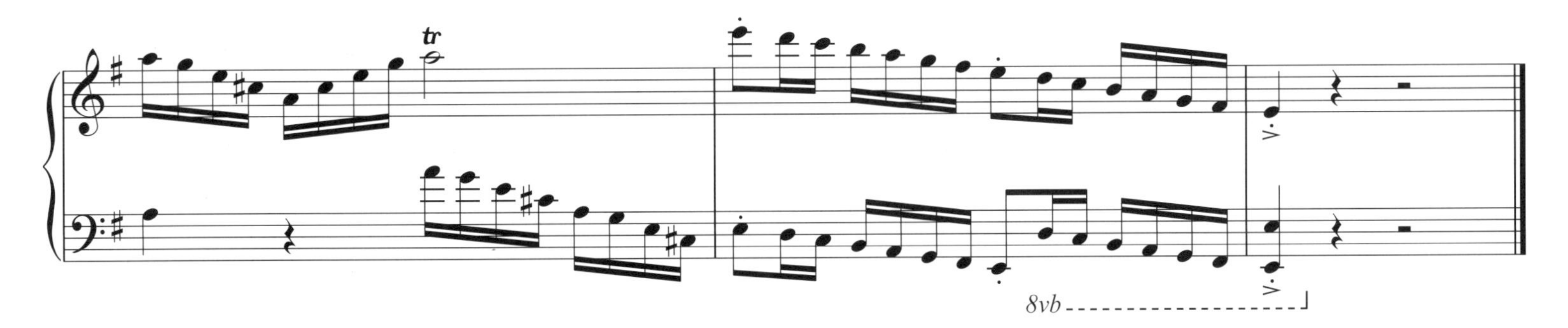

DEAD MEN TELL NO TALES

Music by
GEOFF ZANELLI

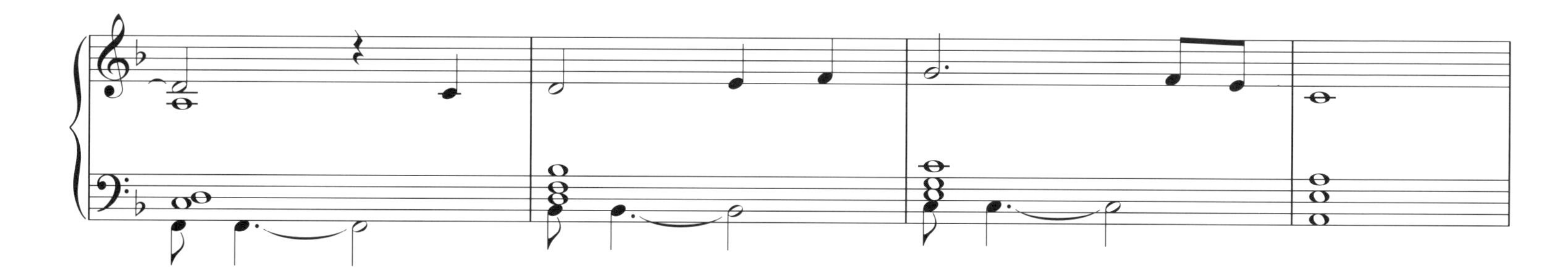

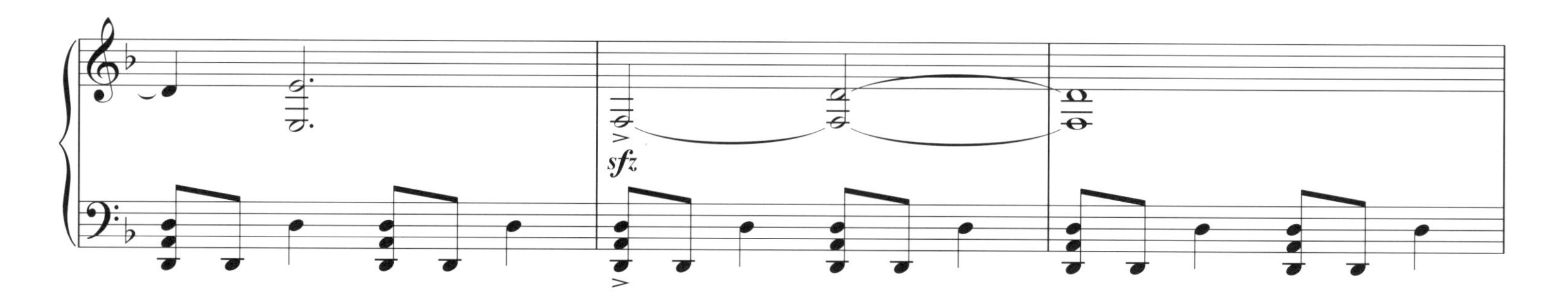

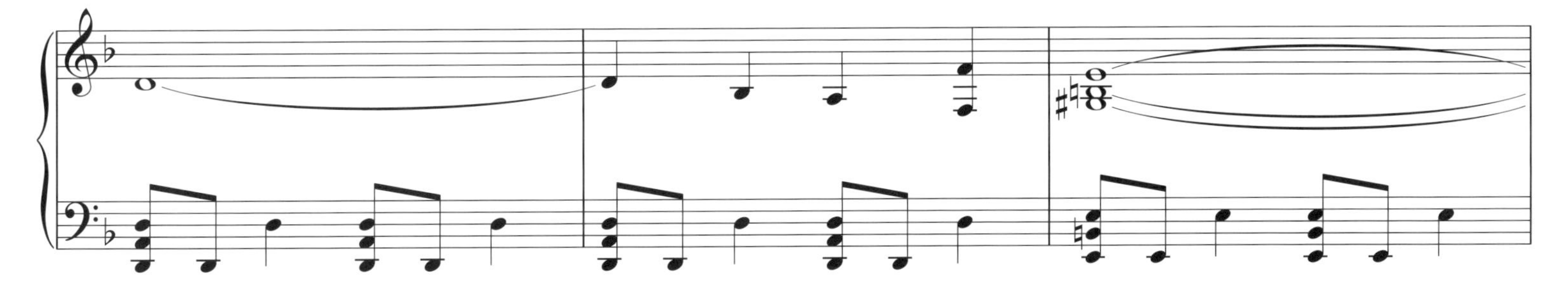

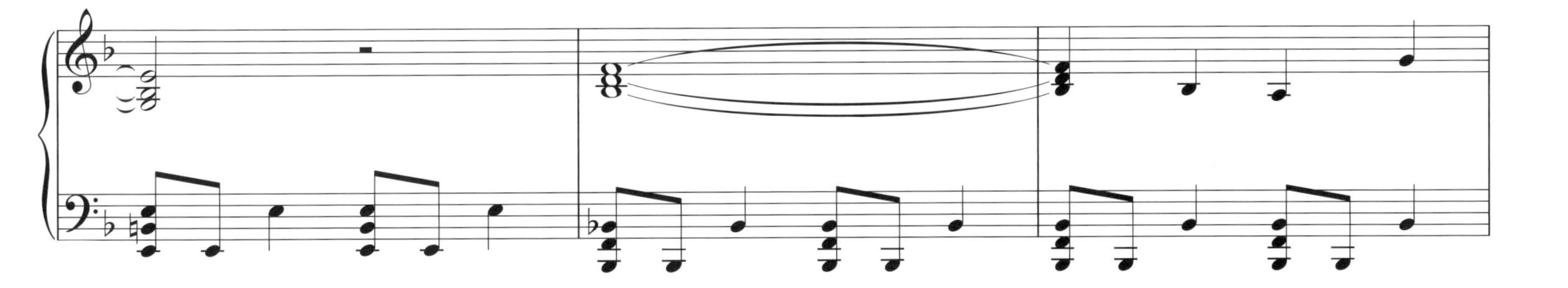

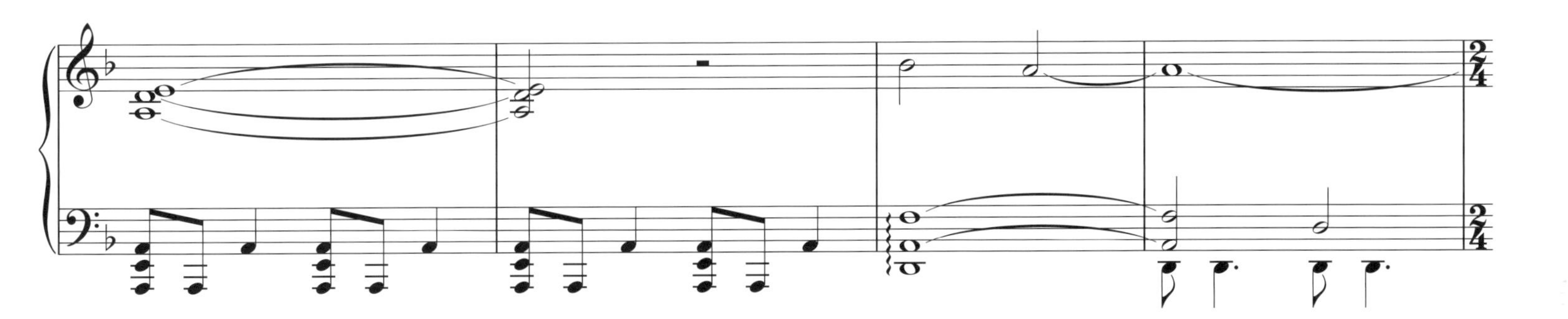

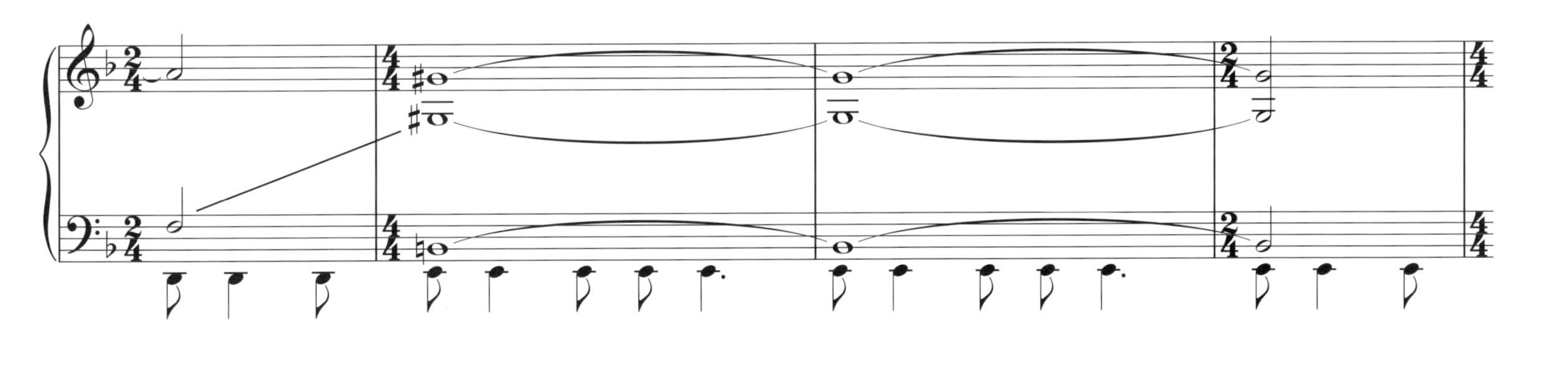

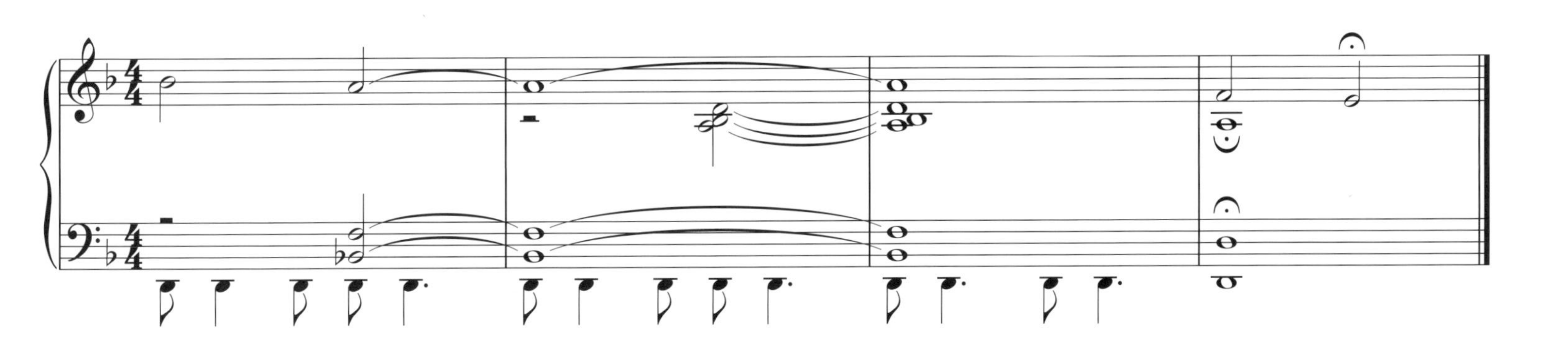

SALAZAR

Music by
GEOFF ZANELLI

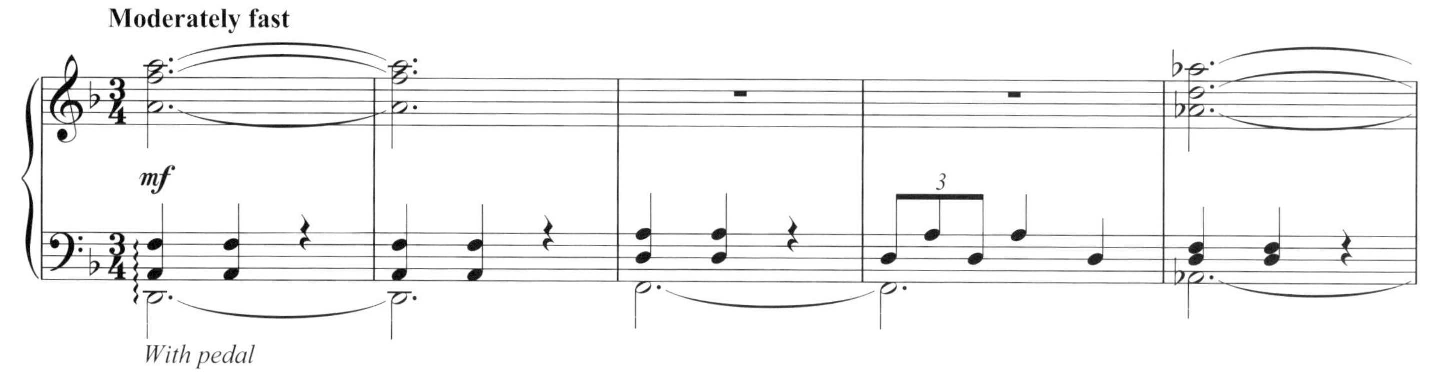

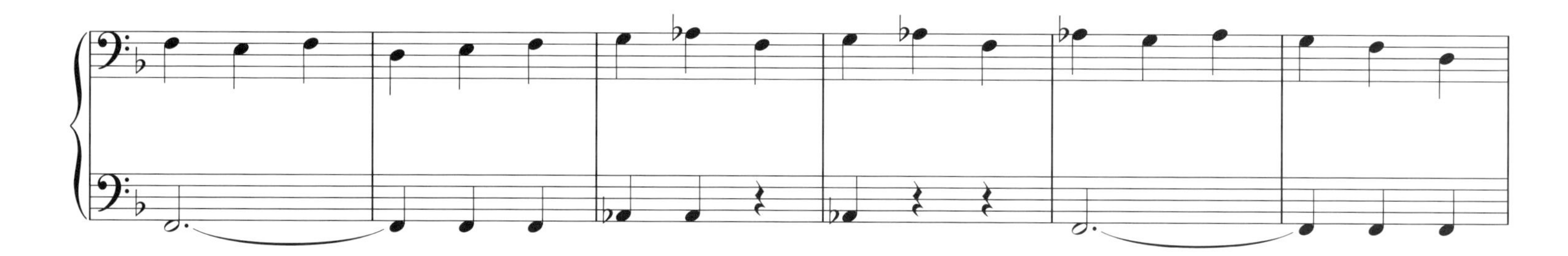

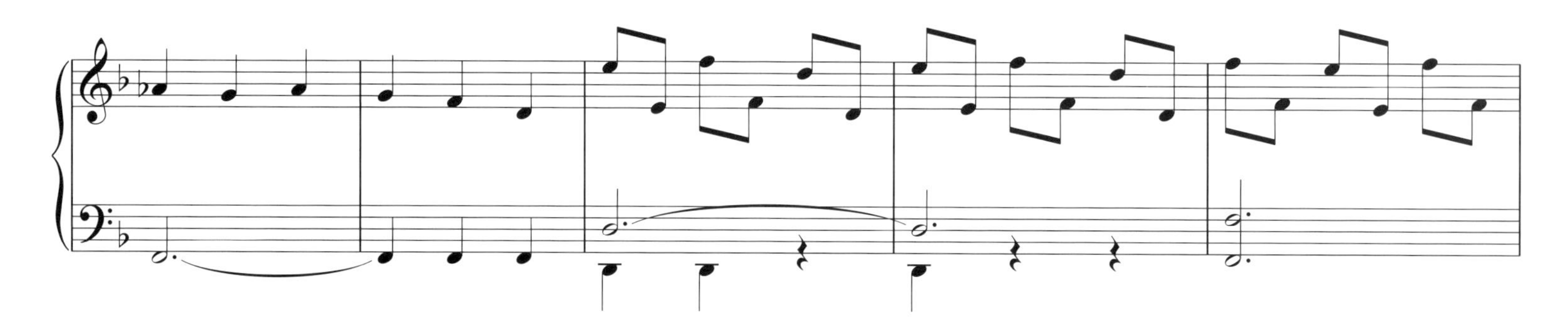

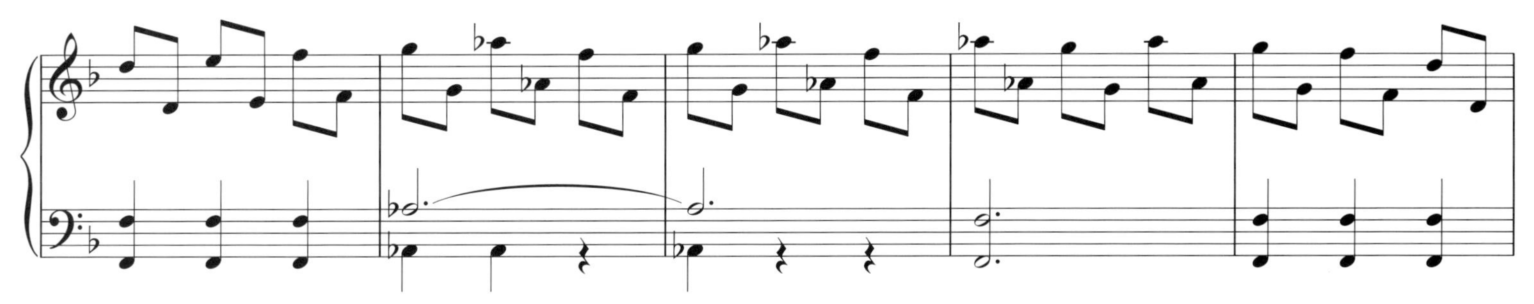

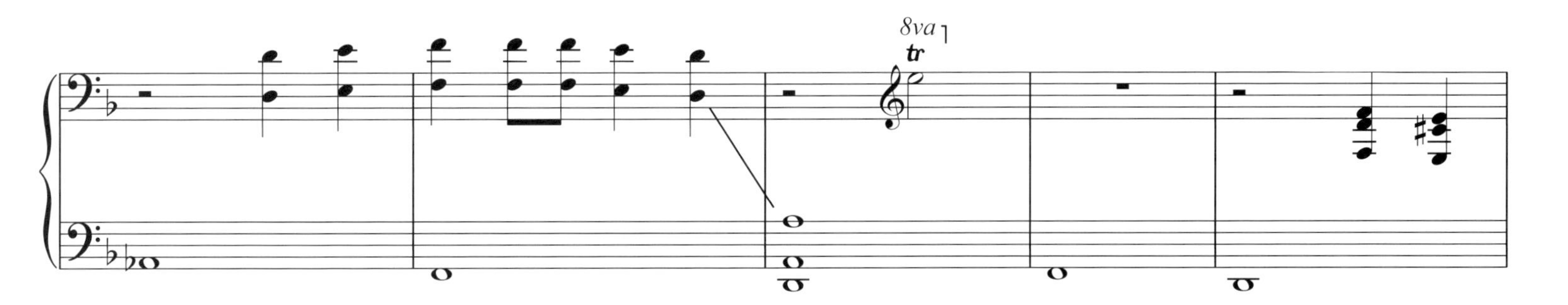

Tempo I

p

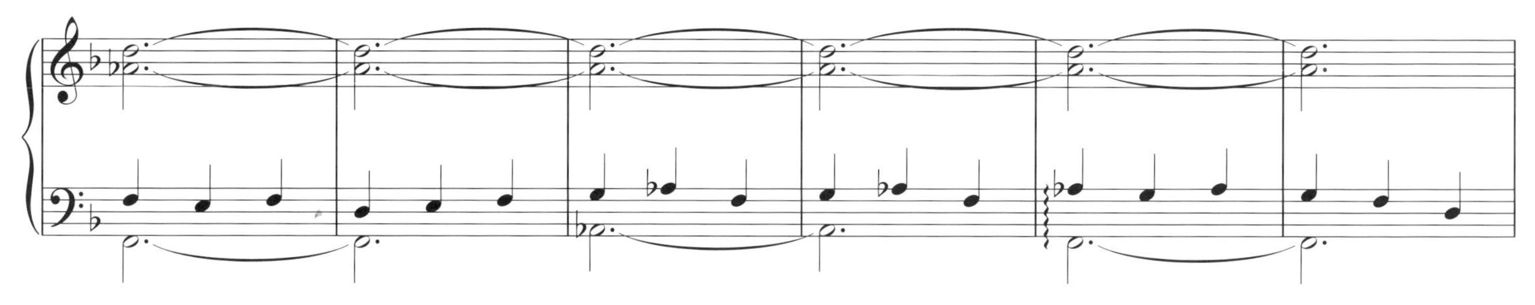

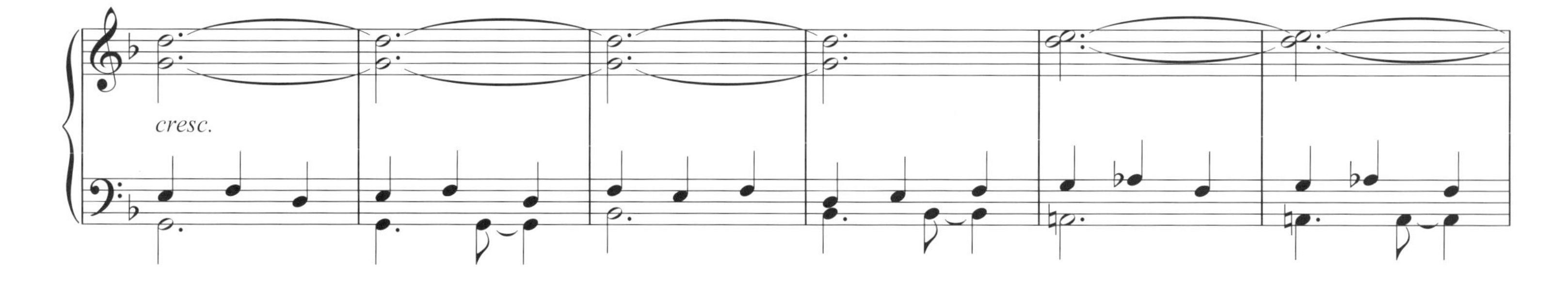
cresc.

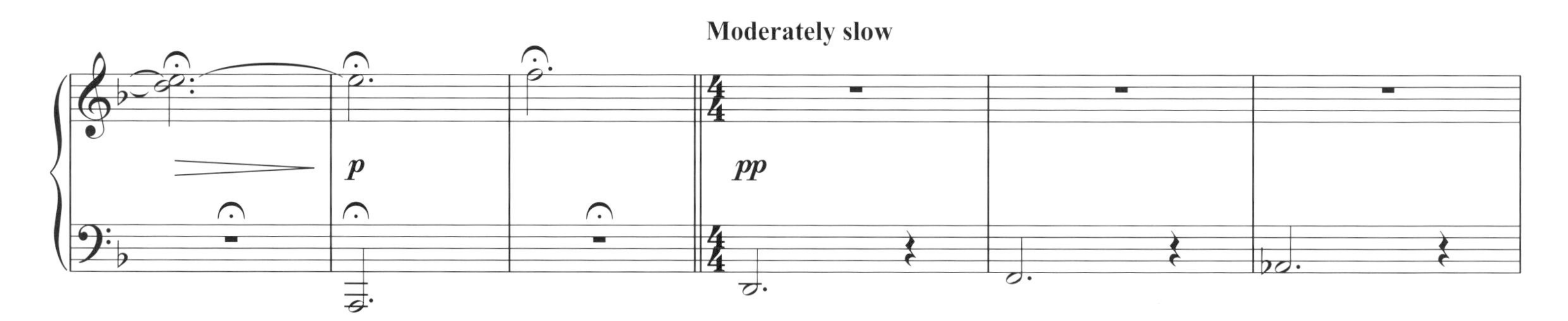
Moderately slow
p
pp

p
8vb

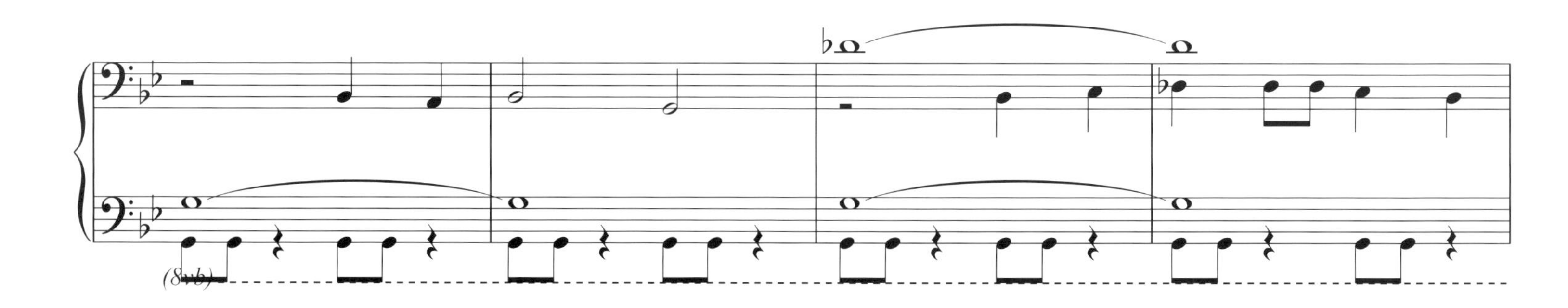
(8vb)

(8vb)
loco

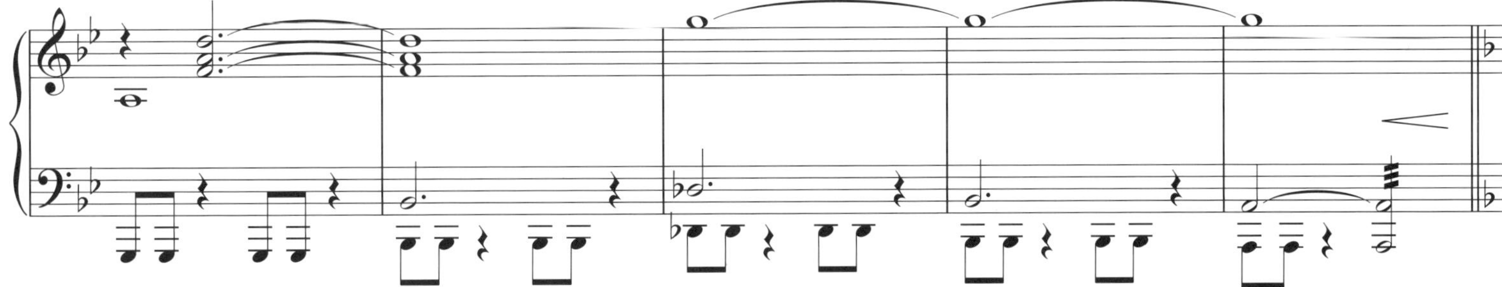

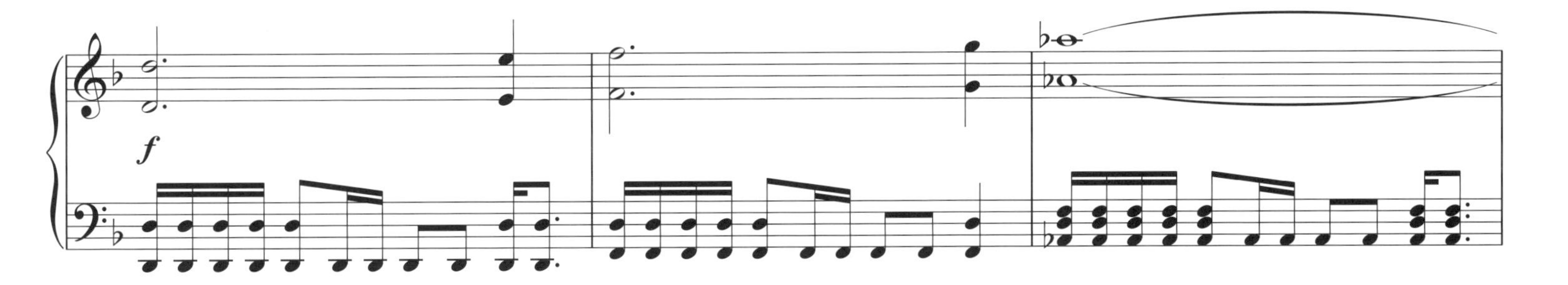
f

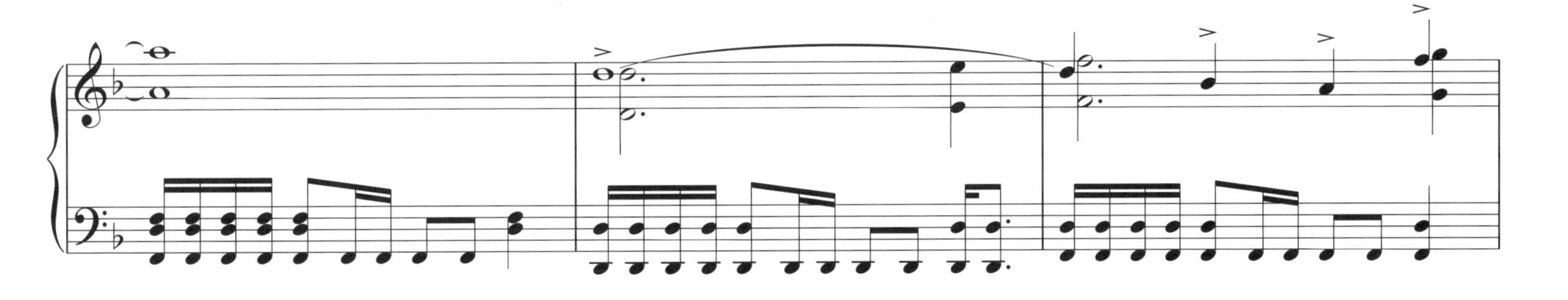

cresc.
ff
mf

NO WOMAN HAS EVER HANDLED MY HERSCHEL

Music by
GEOFF ZANELLI

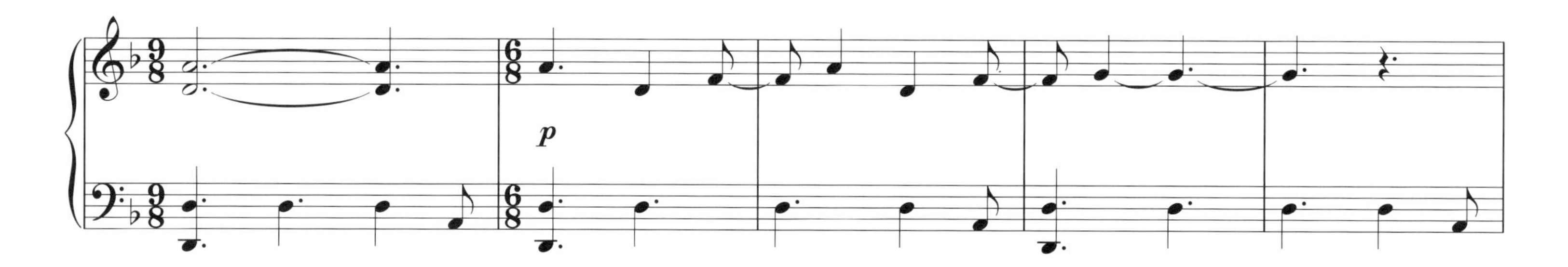

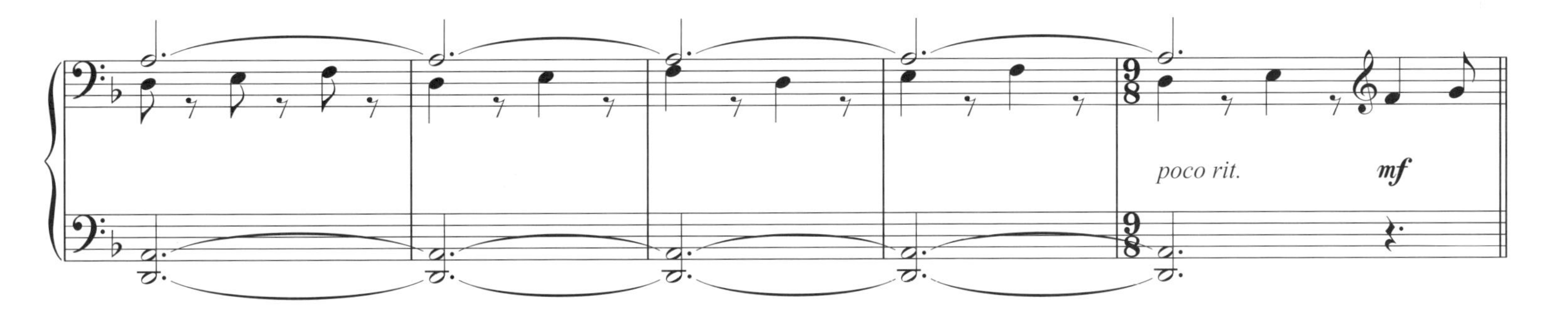

A little slower

Tempo I
mp

sim.

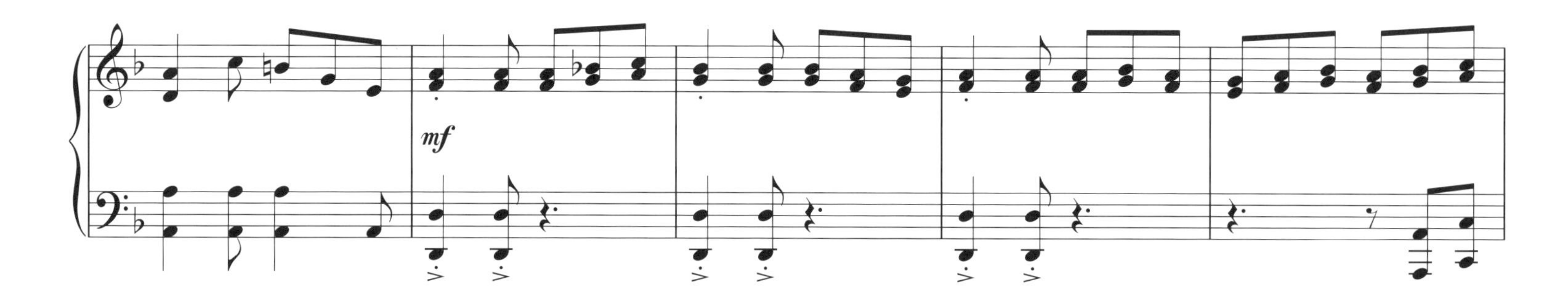
mf

p

mf

mp

R.H.
mf

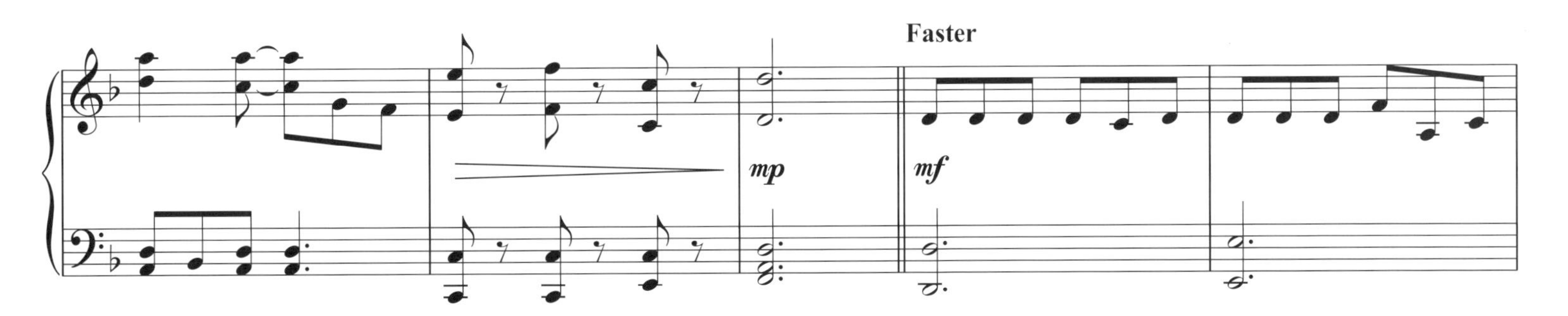
Faster
mp
mf

p
ff

f

ff
f

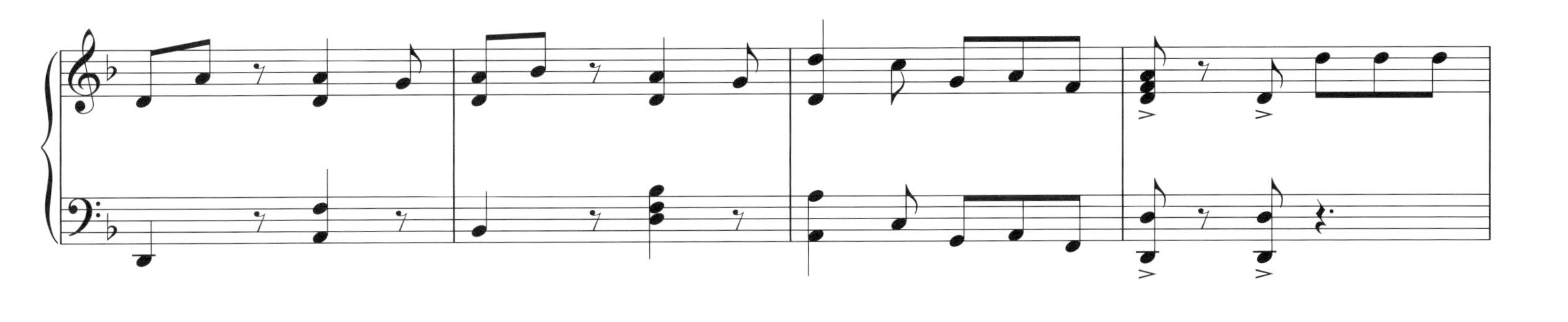

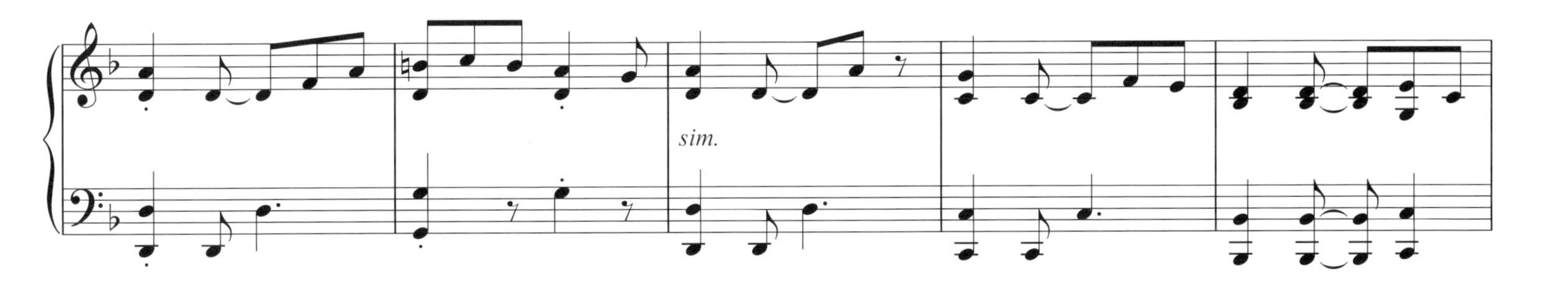
sim.

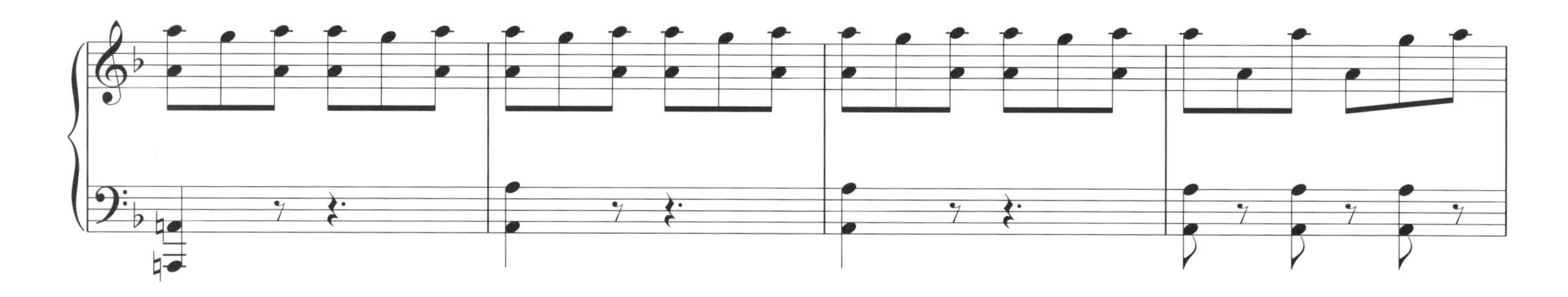

ff

sim.

rall.

YOU SPEAK OF THE TRIDENT

Music by
GEOFF ZANELLI

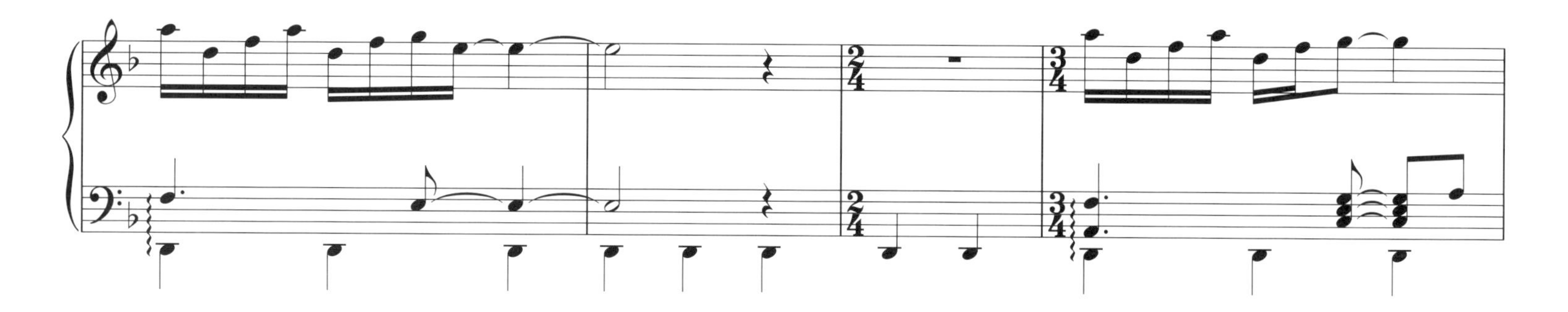

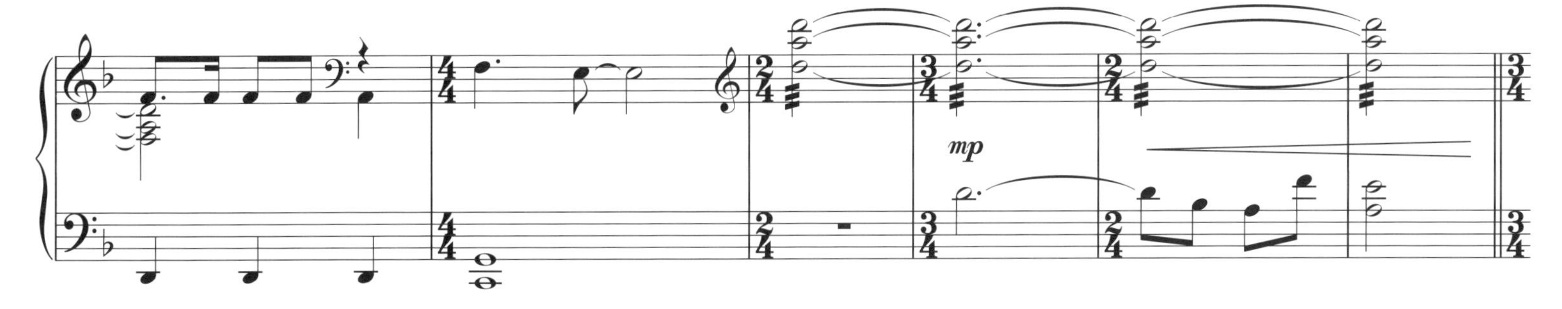
mp

Quickly
f
R.H.

sim.
8vb

(8vb)

(8vb)
loco

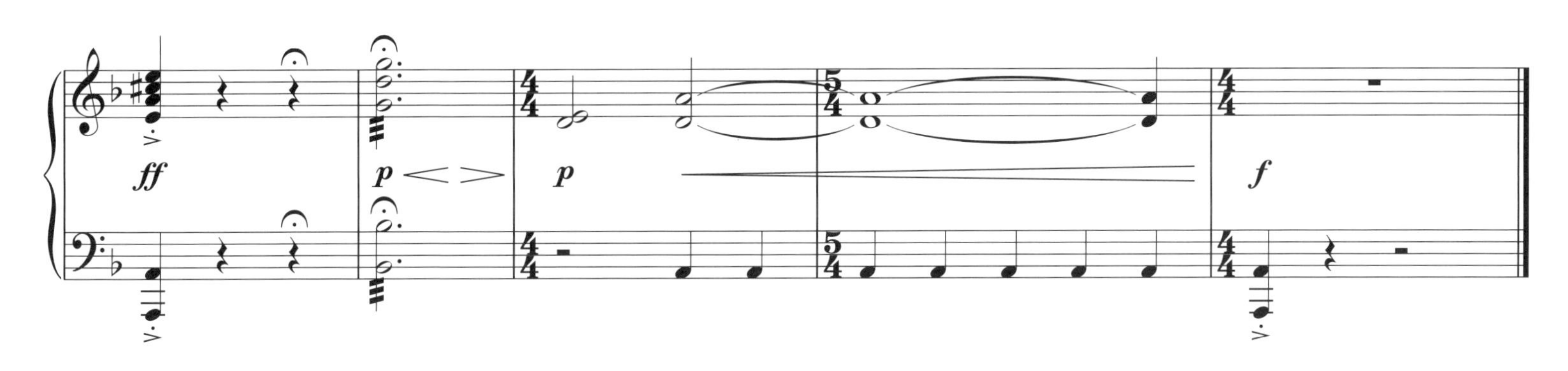
ff
p
p
f

KILL THE FILTHY PIRATE, I'LL WAIT

Music by
GEOFF ZANELLI

Brightly
mf
f

sim.
sim.

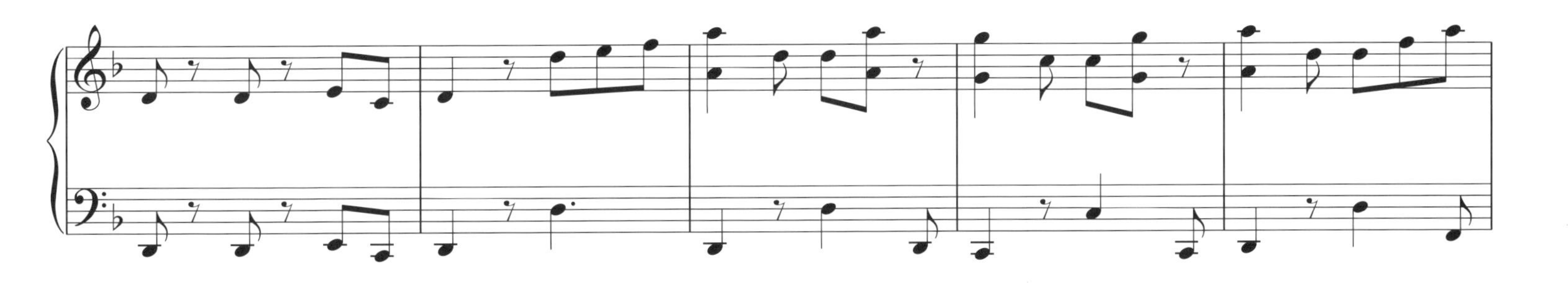

mp

f

mp

f

mp

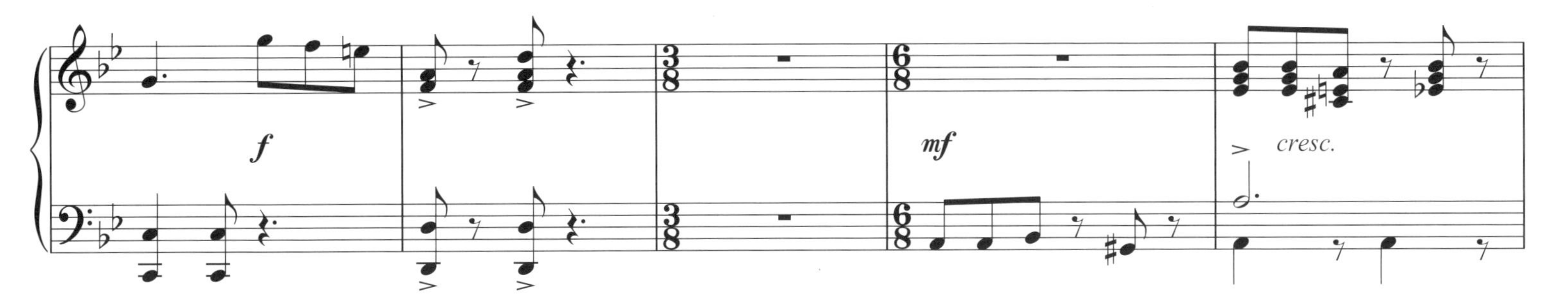
f
mf
cresc.

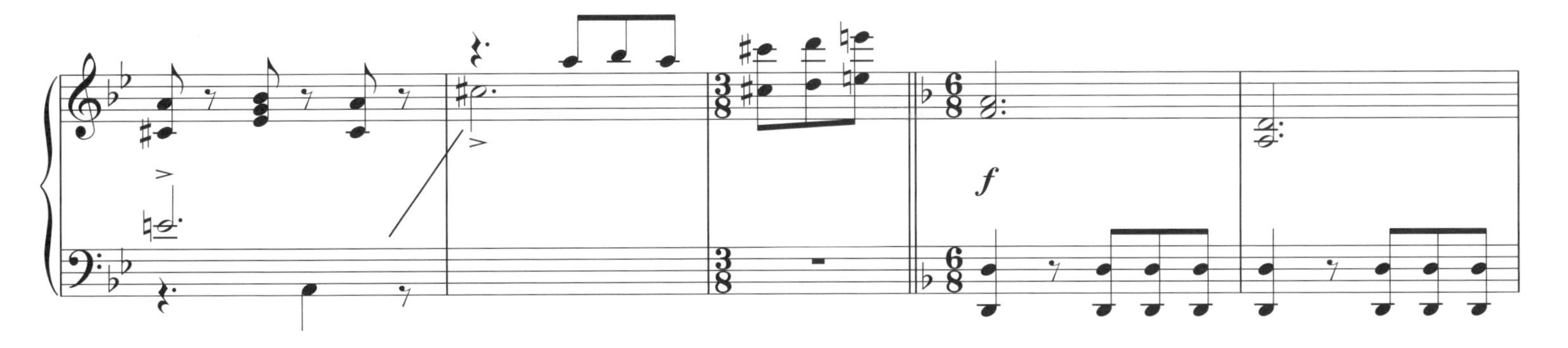
f

ff

mf

mp

p

mf

ff

sim.

accel.

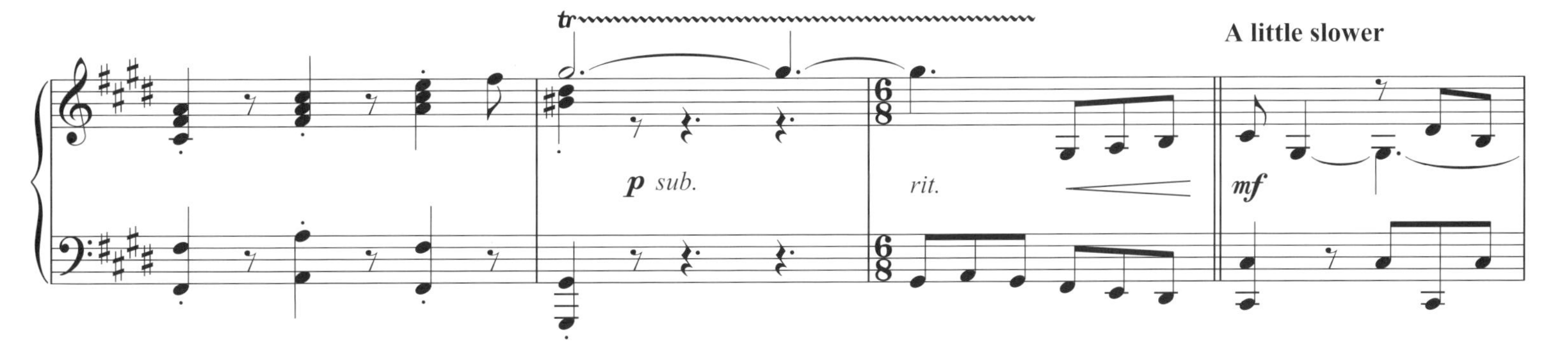
tr
A little slower
p sub.
rit.
mf

(♪ = ♪)

p
sim.

mf
mp

cresc.

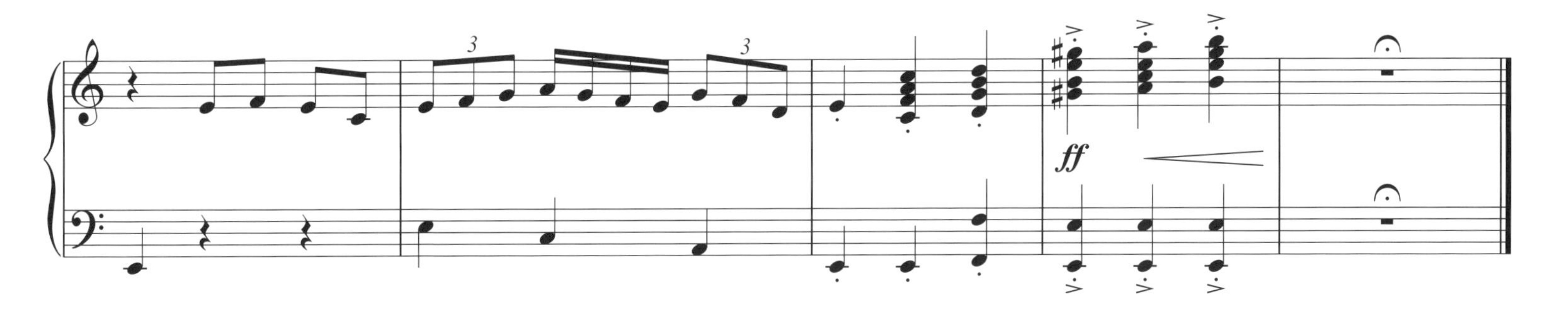
ff

TREASURE

Music by
GEOFF ZANELLI

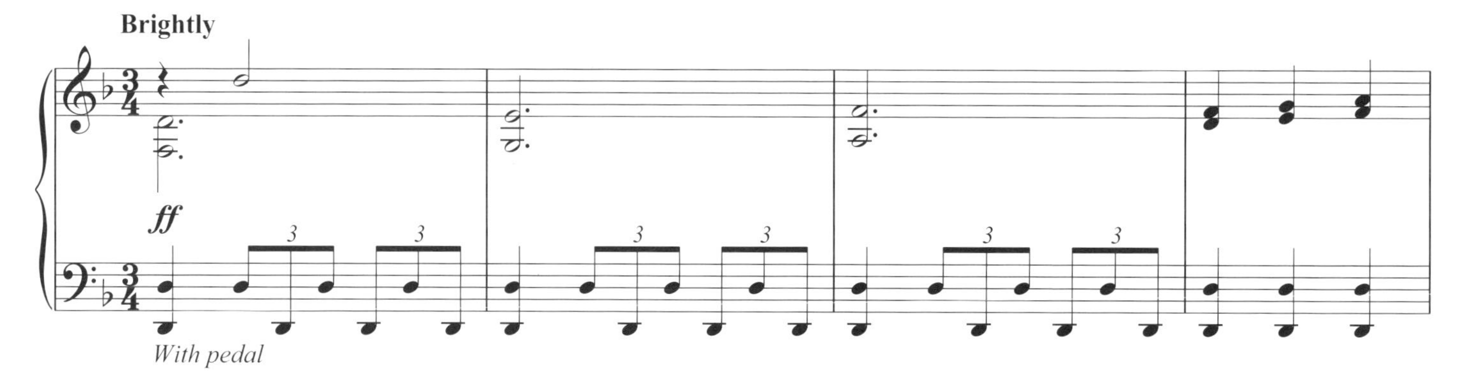

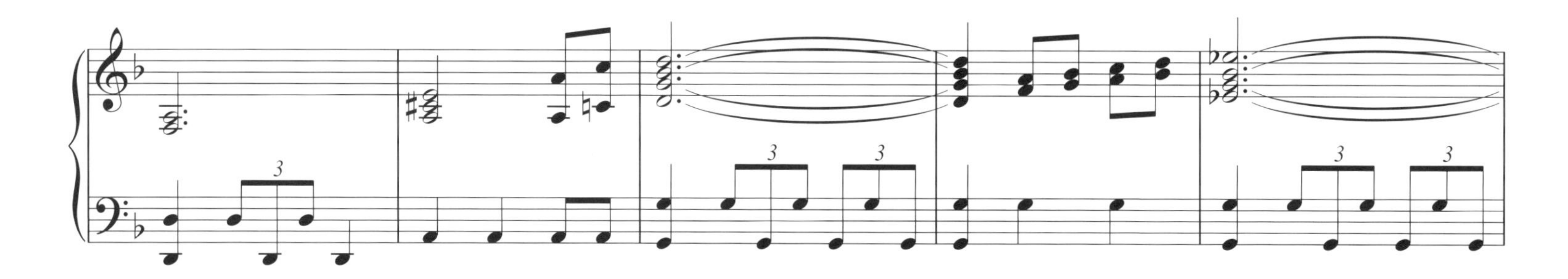

Much faster, in one
f
8vb
(8vb)
mf
sim.
(8vb)
(8vb)
f
(8vb)
3
3

(8vb)
(8vb)
mf
loco
cresc. poco a poco
ff
f

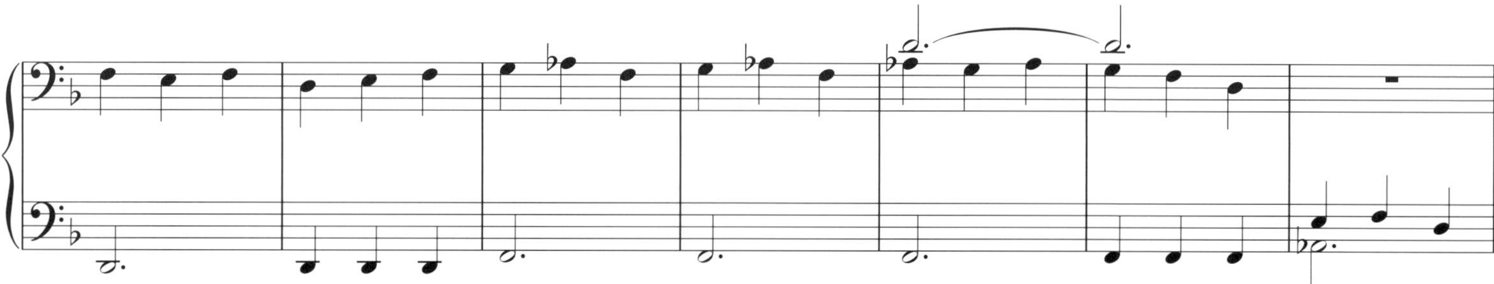

3

cresc.

Suddenly slower
fff

Slowly
f

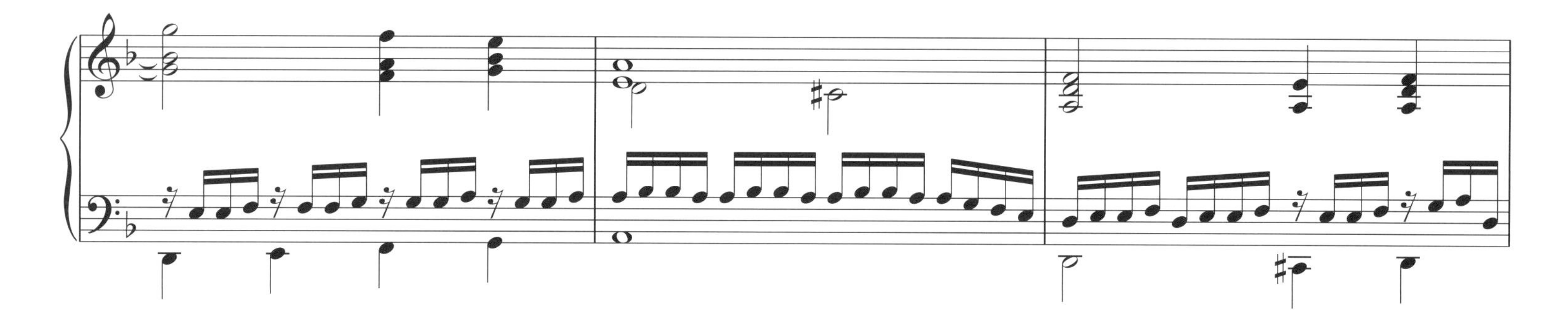

ff

3
8vb

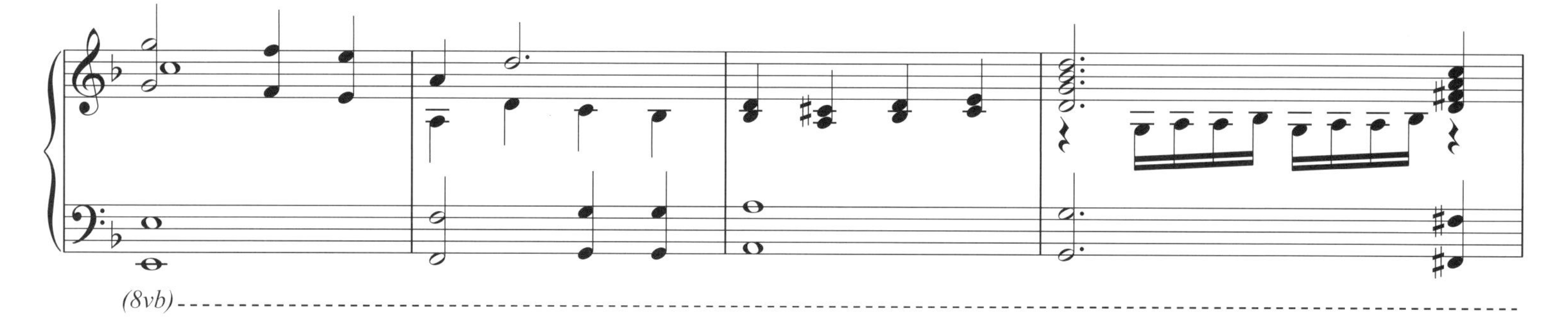
(8vb)

(8vb)

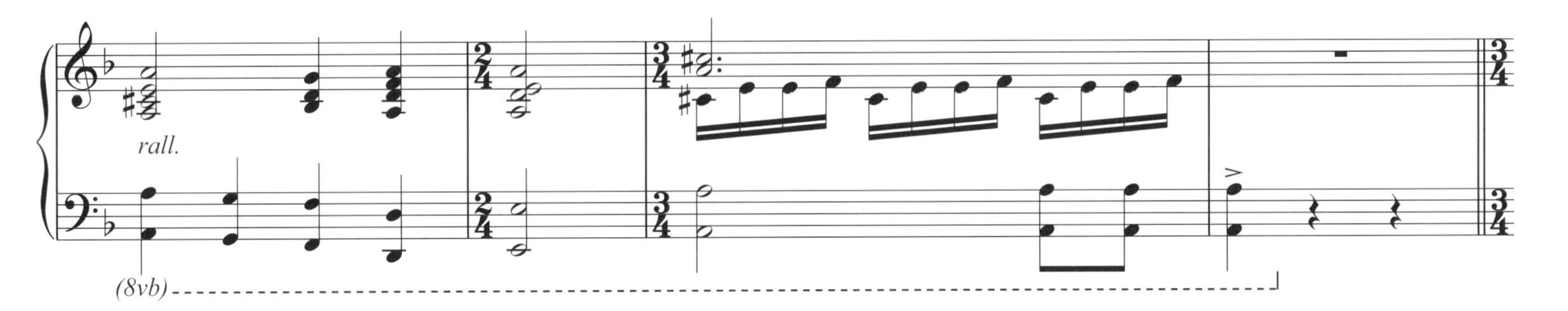
rall.
(8vb)

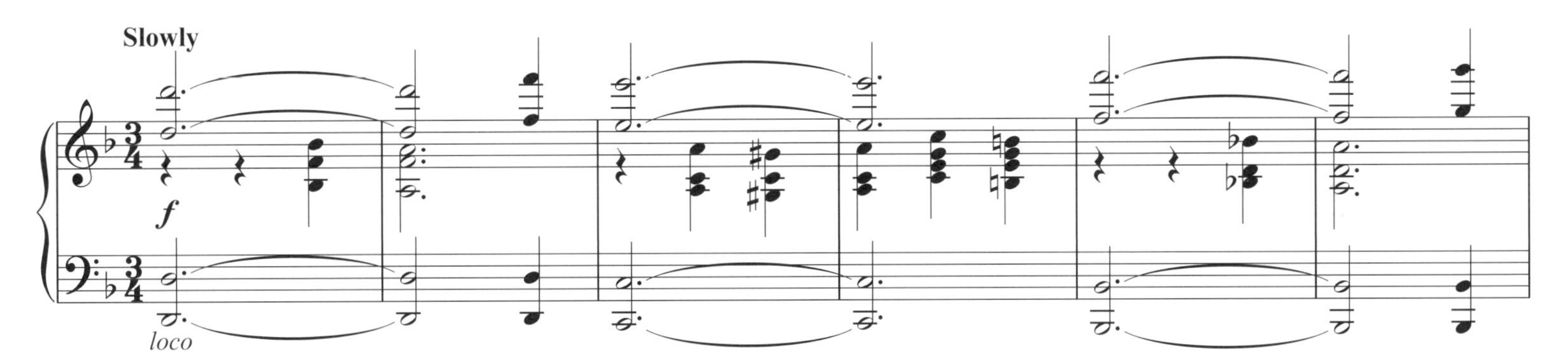
Slowly
f
loco

Moderately slow
accel.

MY NAME IS BARBOSSA

Music by
GEOFF ZANELLI

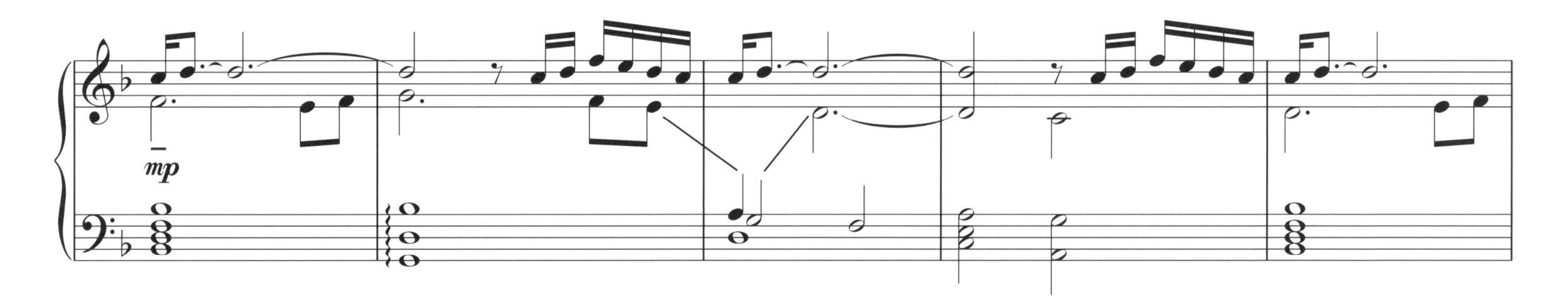

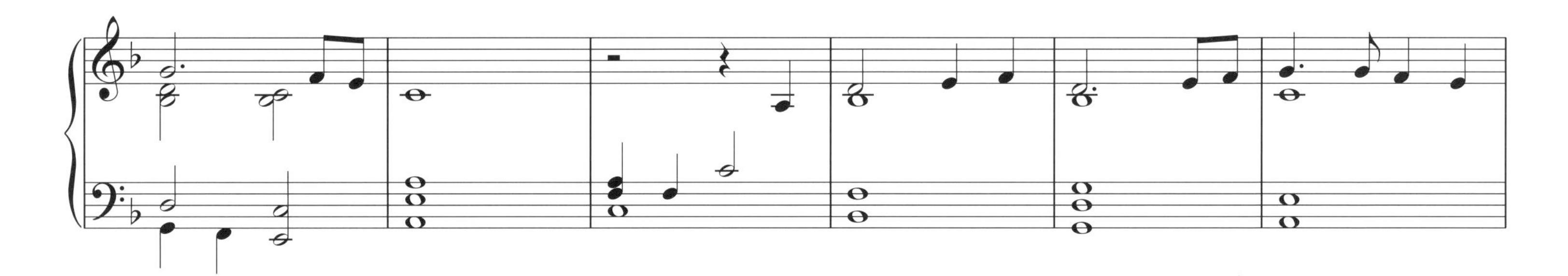

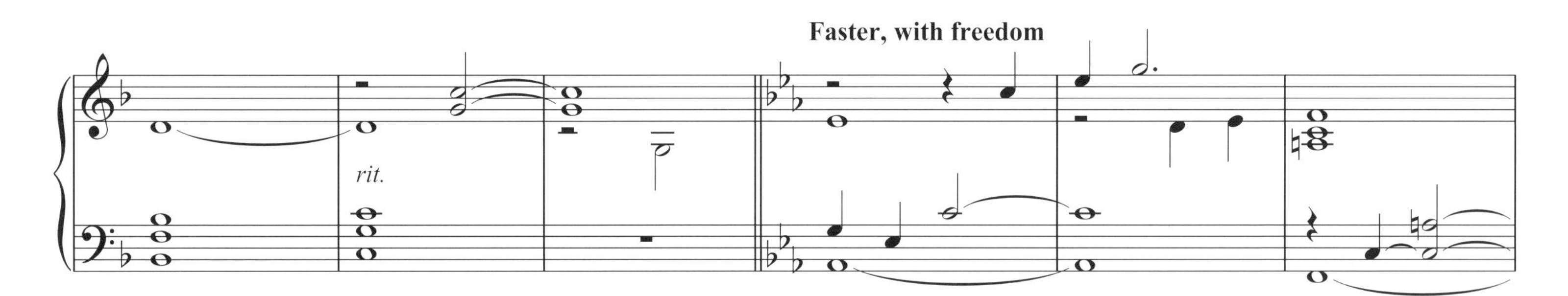

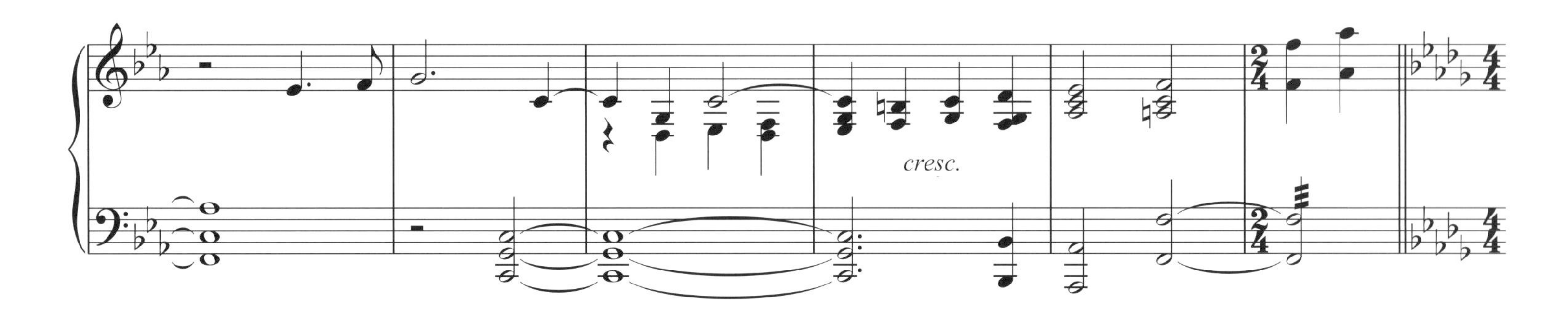

Slowly, with passion

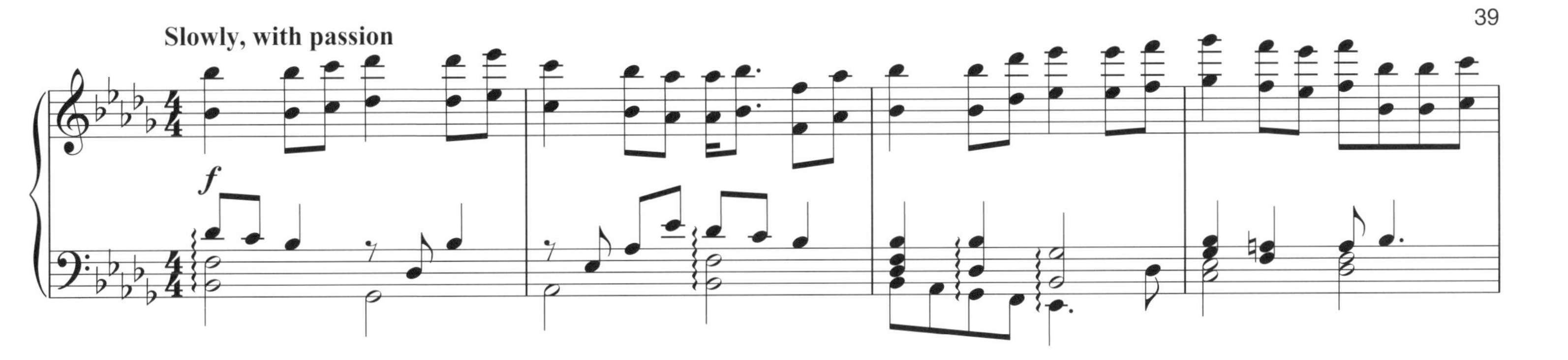

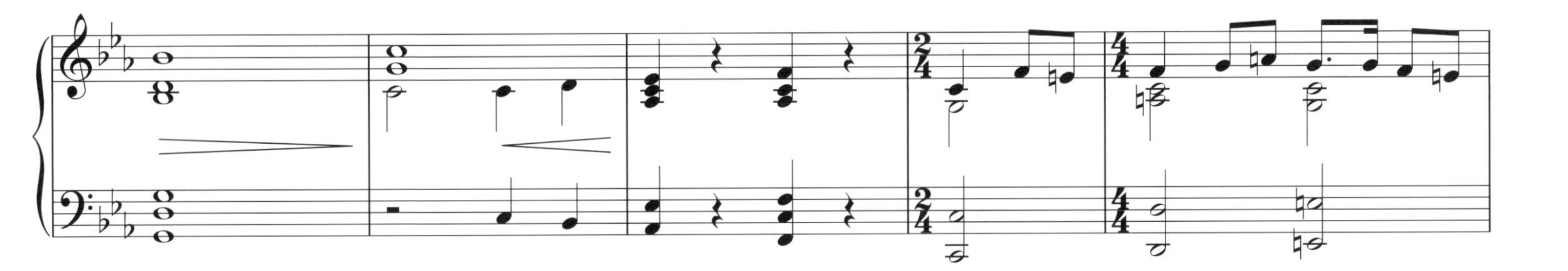

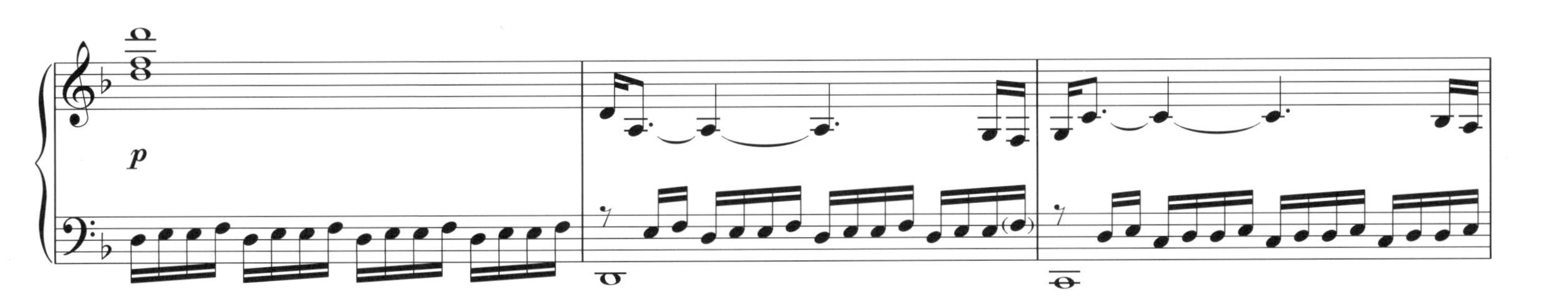

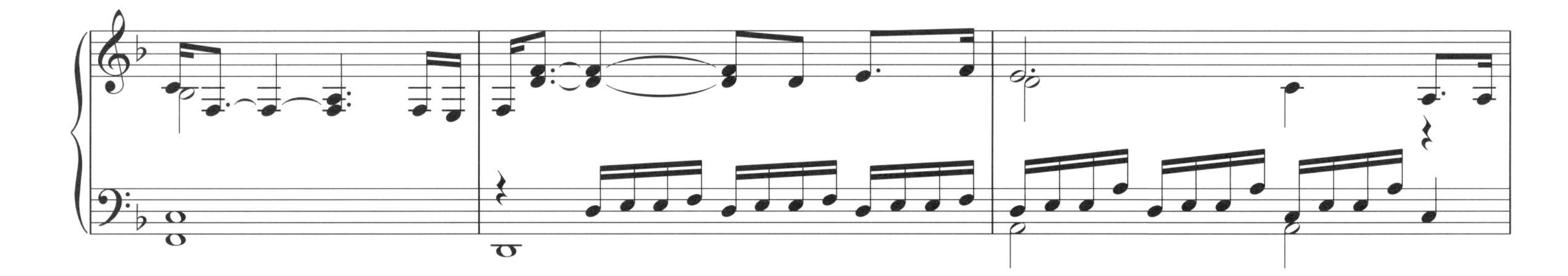

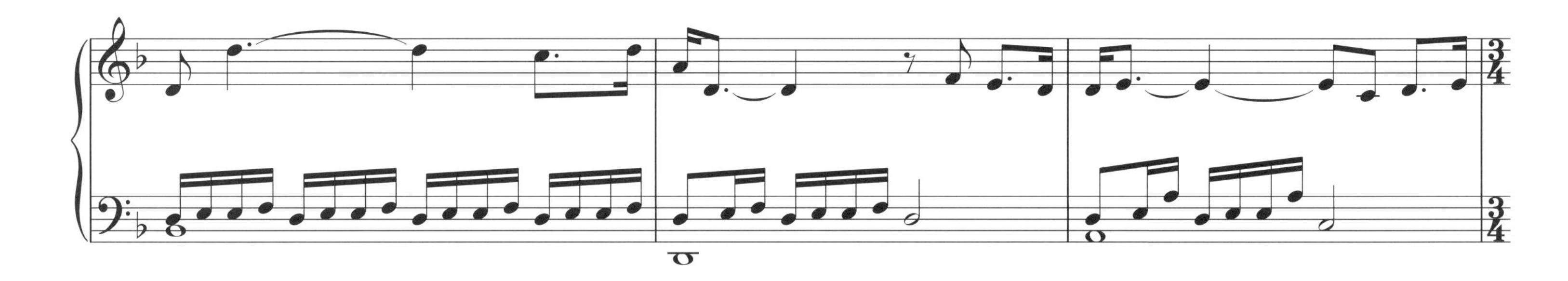

cresc.
mf

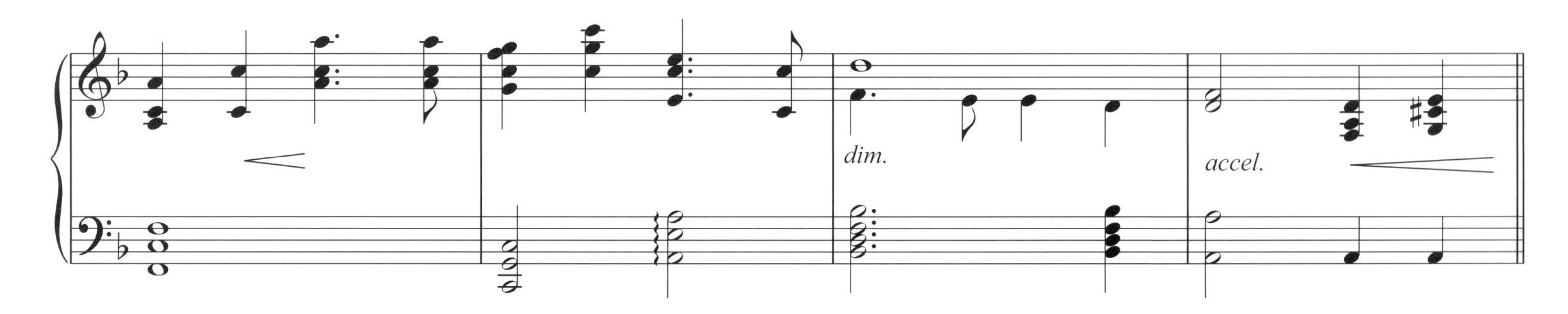
dim.
accel.

Moderately slow
f

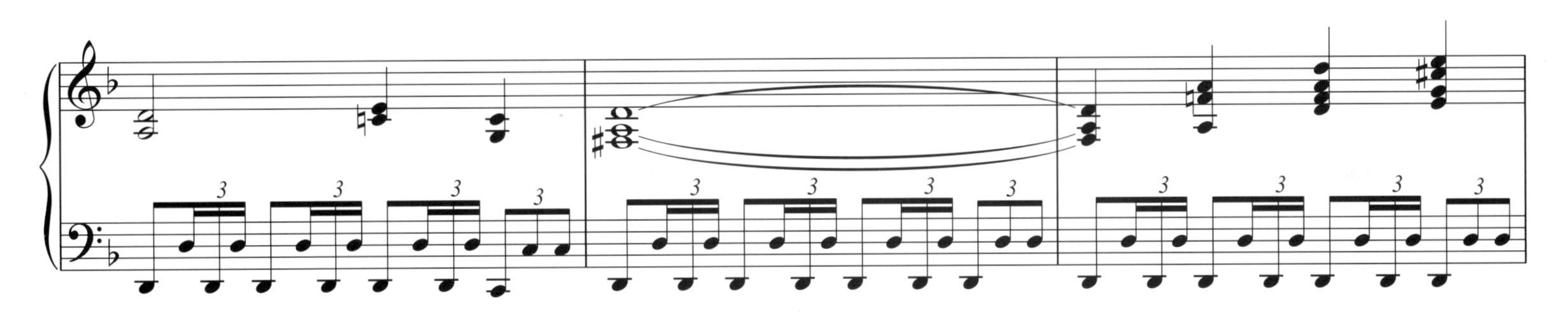

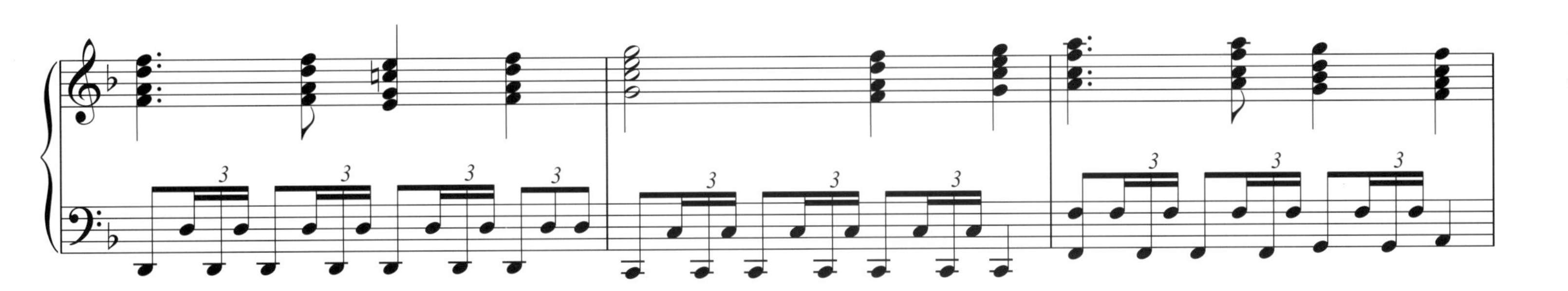

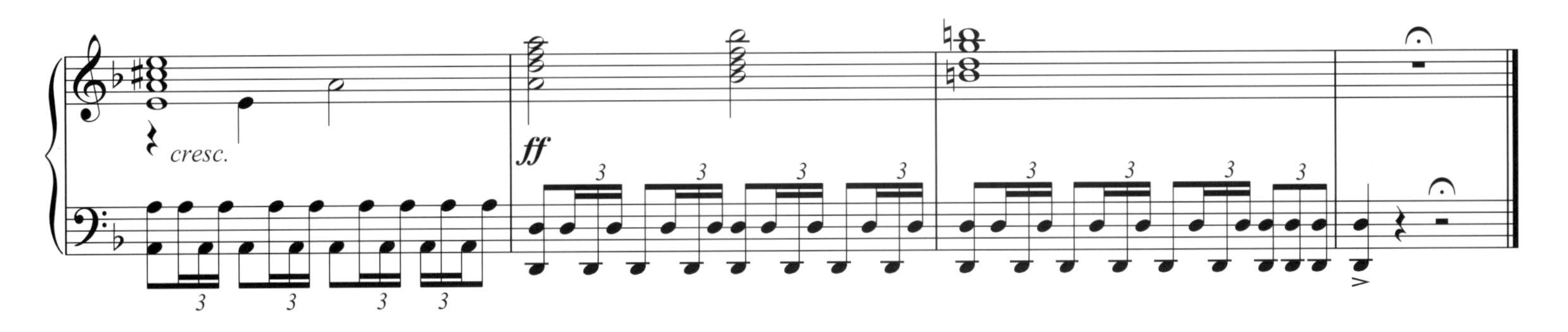
cresc.
ff

BEYOND MY BELOVED HORIZON

Music by
GEOFF ZANELLI

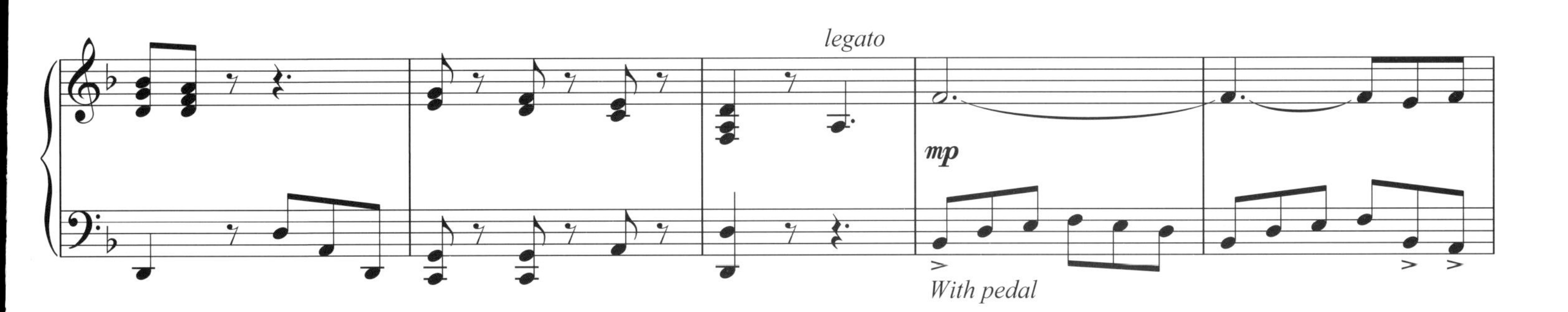
legato
mp
With pedal

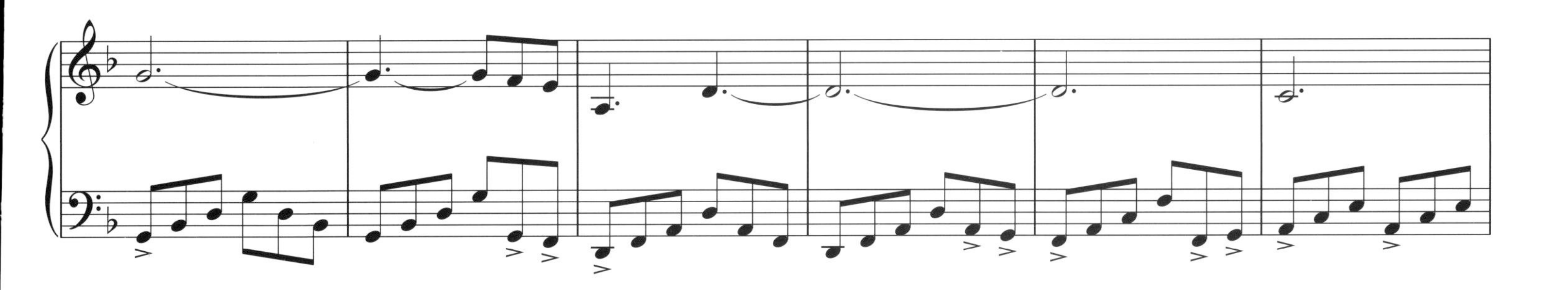

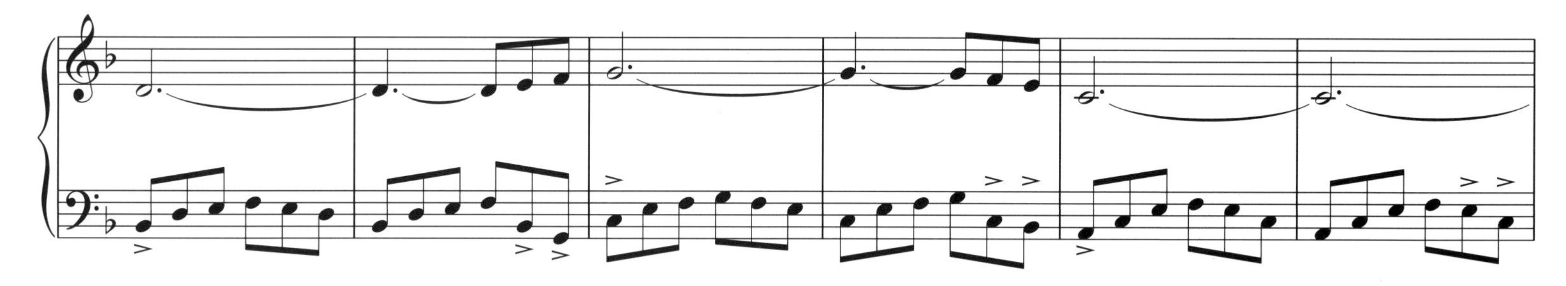

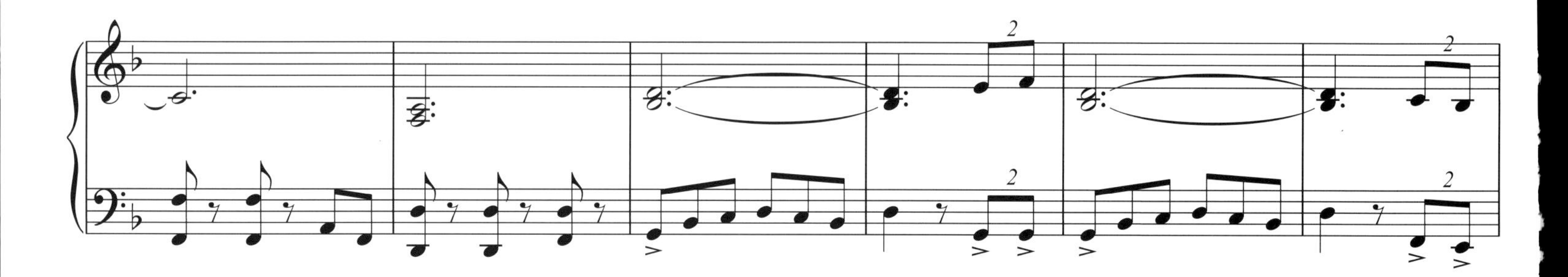

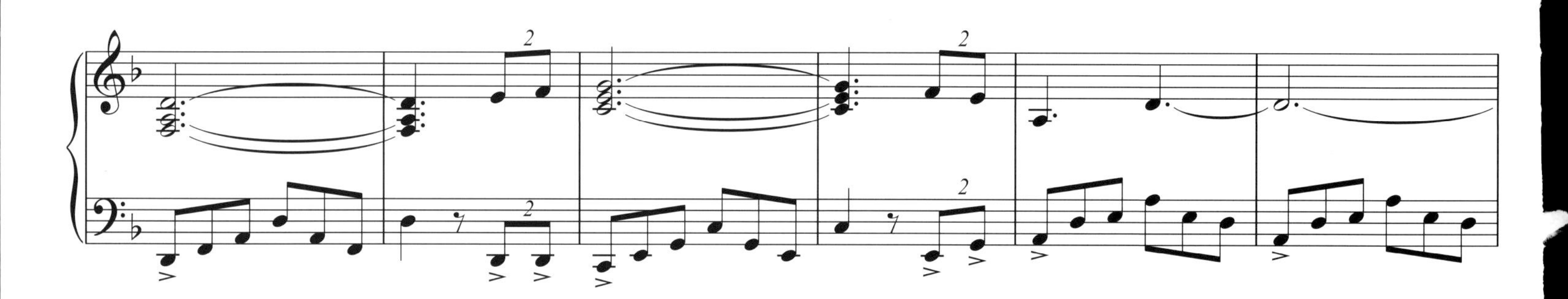

f

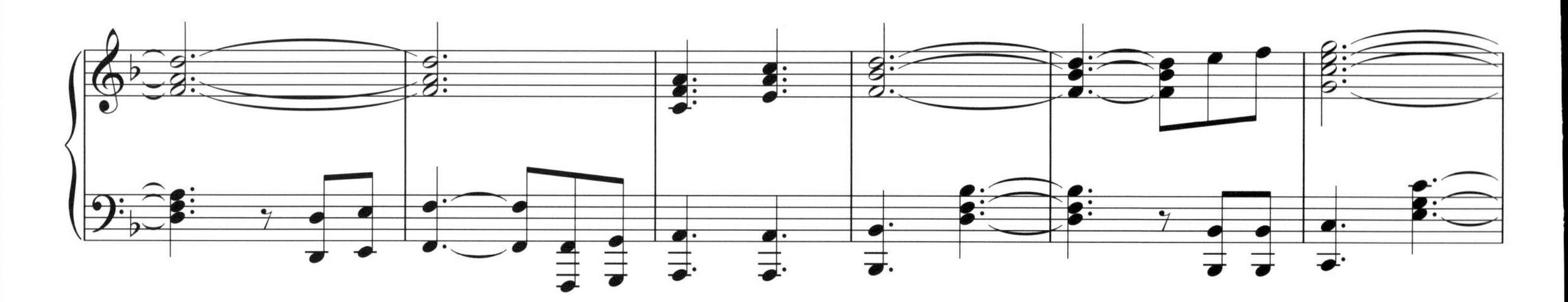

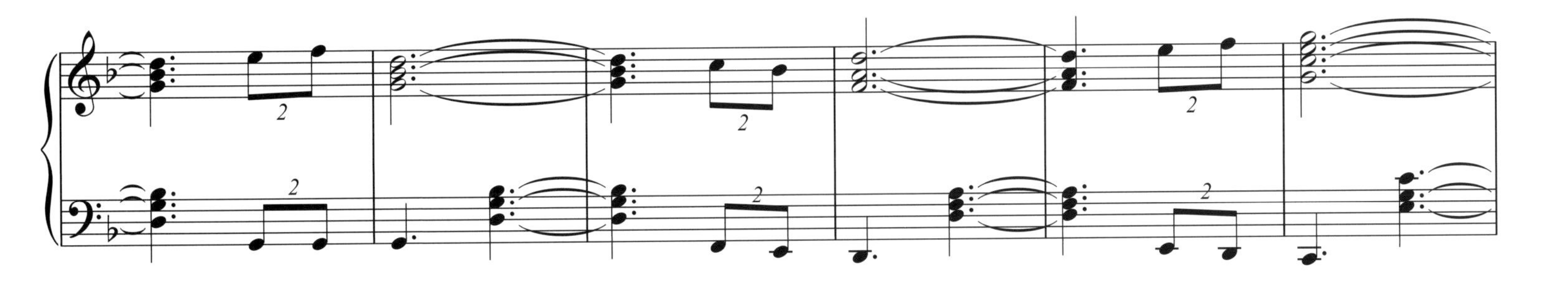

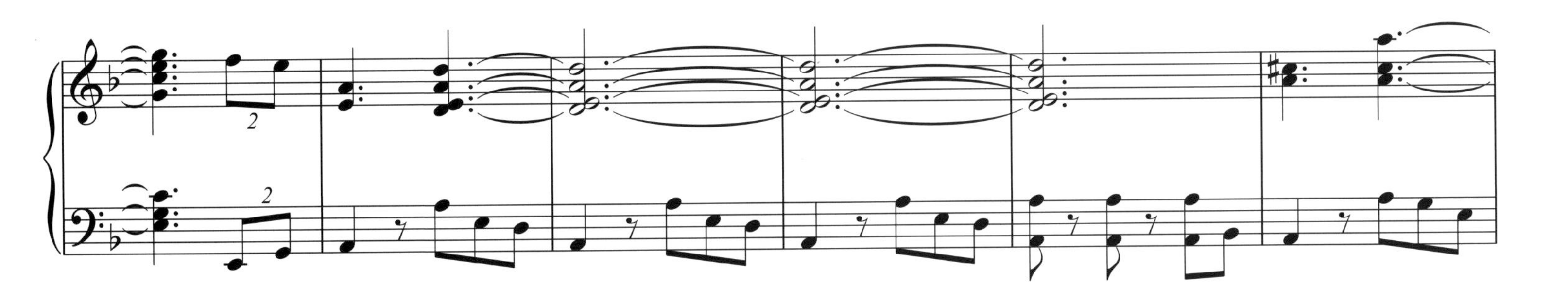

p

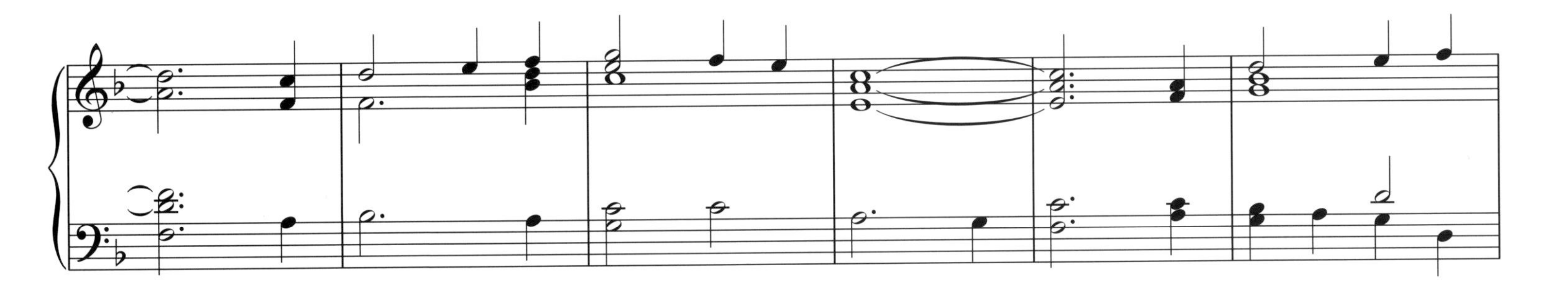

THE BRIGHTEST STAR IN THE NORTH

Music by
GEOFF ZANELLI

Slowly

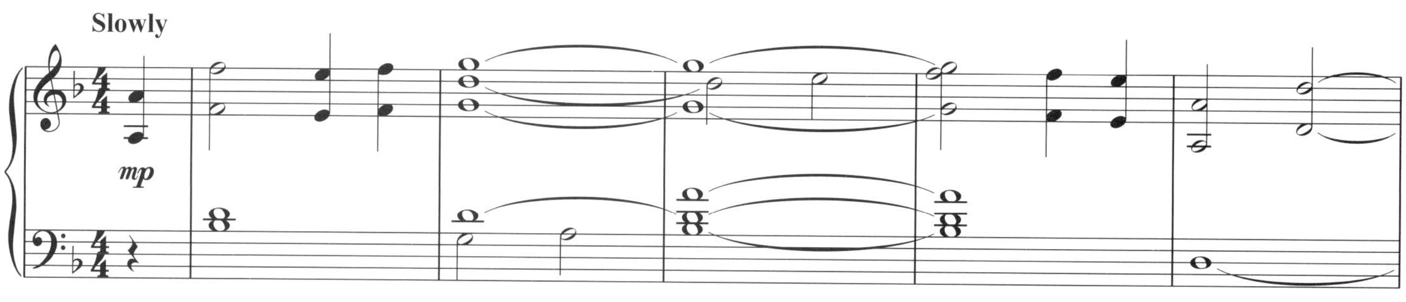

With pedal

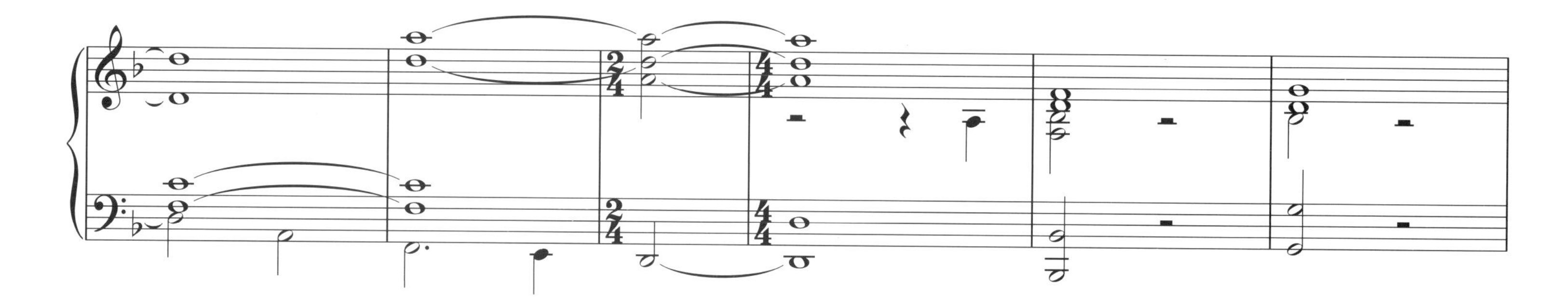

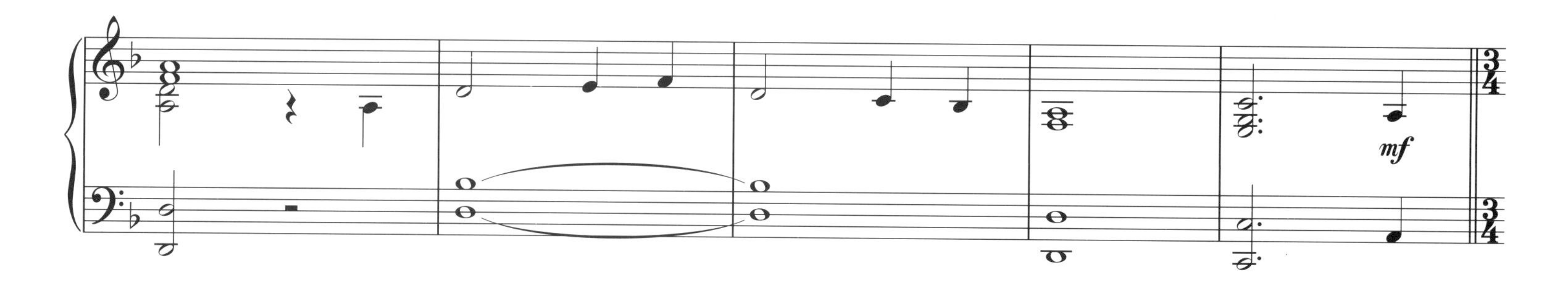

Moving a little faster

p

Broadly
mf

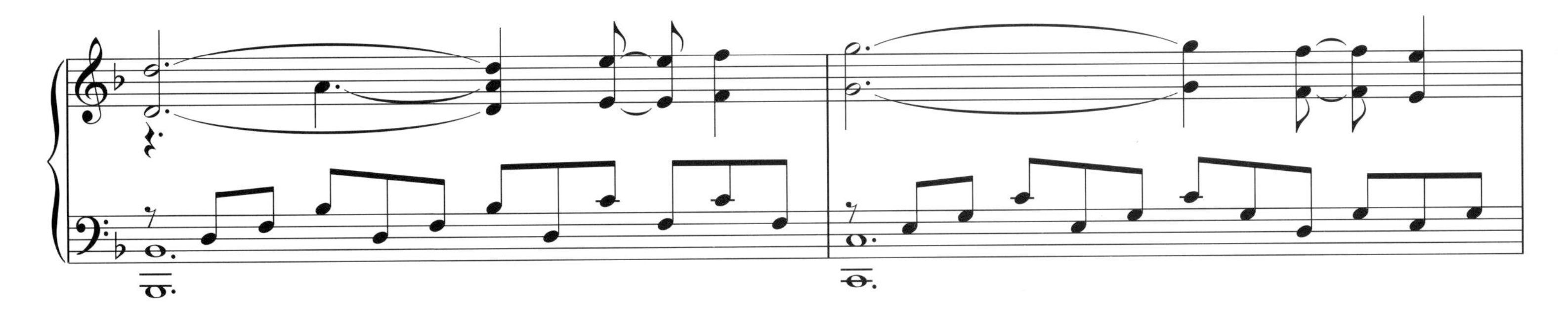

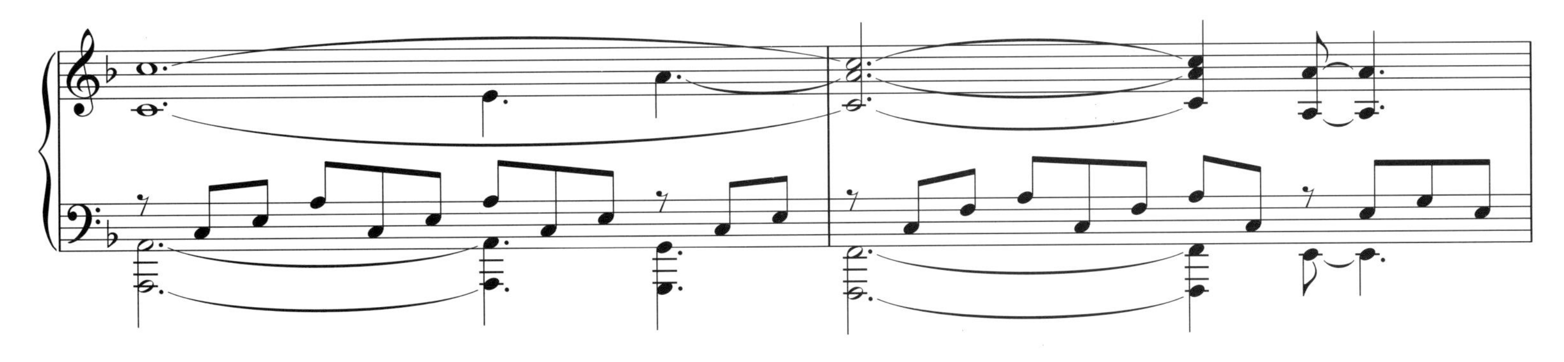

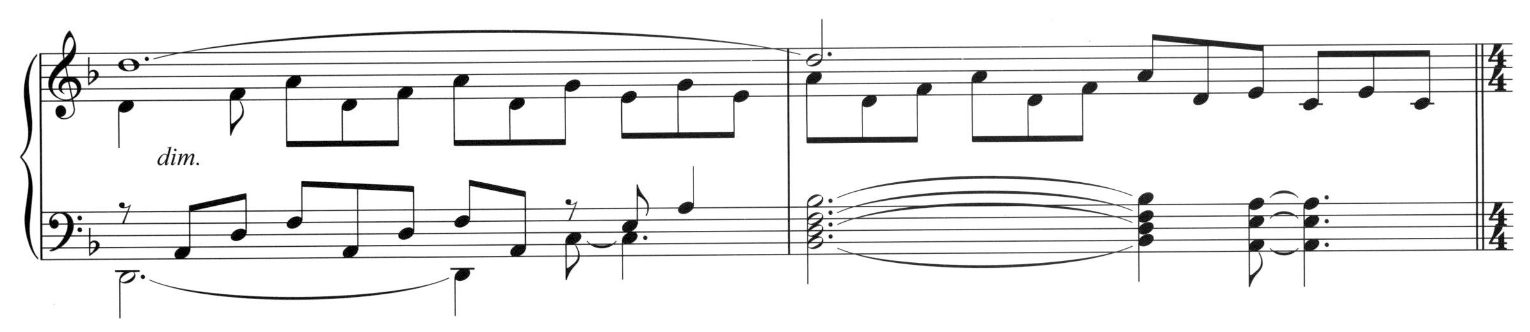
dim.

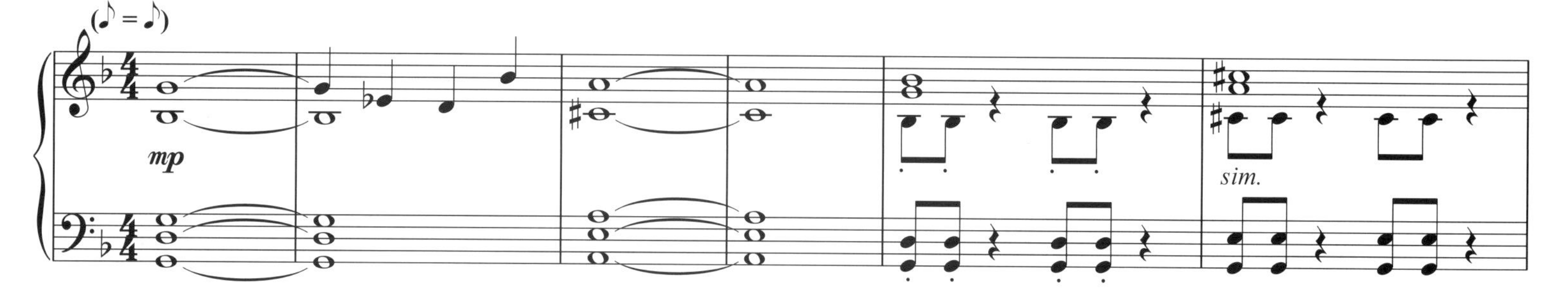
(♪ = ♪)
mp
sim.

(♪ = ♪.)
p

Slower

mp